Bloom's
GUIDES

Richard Wright's
Black Boy

The Adventures of Huckleberry Finn
All the Pretty Horses
Animal Farm
The Autobiography of Malcolm X
The Awakening
The Bell Jar
Beloved
Beowulf
Black Boy
The Bluest Eye
Brave New World
The Canterbury Tales
Catch-22
The Catcher in the Rye
The Chosen
The Crucible
Cry, the Beloved Country
Death of a Salesman
Fahrenheit 451
A Farewell to Arms
Frankenstein
The Glass Menagerie
The Grapes of Wrath
Great Expectations
The Great Gatsby
Hamlet
The Handmaid's Tale
Heart of Darkness
The House on Mango Street
I Know Why the Caged Bird Sings
The Iliad
Invisible Man
Jane Eyre

The Joy Luck Club
The Kite Runner
Lord of the Flies
Macbeth
Maggie: A Girl of the Streets
The Member of the Wedding
The Metamorphosis
Native Son
Night
1984
The Odyssey
Oedipus Rex
Of Mice and Men
One Hundred Years of Solitude
Pride and Prejudice
Ragtime
A Raisin in the Sun
The Red Badge of Courage
Romeo and Juliet
The Scarlet Letter
A Separate Peace
Slaughterhouse-Five
Snow Falling on Cedars
The Stranger
A Streetcar Named Desire
The Sun Also Rises
A Tale of Two Cities
Their Eyes Were Watching God
The Things They Carried
To Kill a Mockingbird
Uncle Tom's Cabin
The Waste Land
Wuthering Heights

Bloom's
GUIDES

Richard Wright's
Black Boy

Edited & with an Introduction
by Harold Bloom

BLOOM'S
LITERARY CRITICISM
An imprint of Infobase Publishing

Bloom's Guides: Black Boy

Copyright © 2010 by Infobase Publishing
Introduction © 2010 by Harold Bloom

Bloom's Literary Criticism
An imprint of Infobase Publishing
132 West 31st Street
New York, NY 10001

Library of Congress Cataloging-in-Publication Data
Bloom, Harold.
  Black boy / by Harold Bloom.
    p. cm.—(Bloom's guides)
  Includes bibliographical references and index.
  ISBN 978-1-60413-575-6
  1. Wright, Richard, 1908–1960.Black boy. I. Title.
  PS3545.R815Z5217 2010
  813'.52—dc22
                            2009030784

Bloom's Literary Criticism books are available at special discounts when purchased in bulk quantities for businesses, associations, institutions, or sales promotions. Please call our Special Sales Department in New York at (212) 967–8800 or (800) 322–8755.

You can find Bloom's Literary Criticism on the World Wide Web at http://www.chelseahouse.com

Contributing editor: Portia Williams Weiskel
Cover design by Takeshi Takahashi
Composition by IBT Global, Troy NY
Cover printed by IBT Global, Troy NY
Book printed and bound by IBT Global, Troy NY
Date printed: December, 2009
Printed in the United States of America

10 9 8 7 6 5 4 3 2 1

This book is printed on acid-free paper.

All links and Web addresses were checked and verified to be correct at the time of publication. Because of the dynamic nature of the Web, some addresses and links may have changed since publication and may no longer be valid.

Contents

120422

Introduction

HAROLD BLOOM

I remember reading *Black Boy: A Record of Childhood and Youth* when Wright's autobiographical book first appeared, in 1945. A boy of fifteen, I was frightened and impressed by the book. Reading it again many years later, the old reactions do not return. Instead, I am compelled to ask the Nietzschean question: Who is the interpreter, and what power does he seek to gain over the text, whether it be his own text or the text of his life? Wright, an anguished and angry interpreter, wrote a far more political work in *Black Boy* than in *Native Son*. What passes for a Marxist analysis of the relation between society and Bigger Thomas seems to me always a kind of authorial afterthought in *Native Son*. In *Black Boy*, this pseudo-Marxism usurps the narrator's function, and the will to power over interpretation becomes the incessant undersong of the entire book. Contrast the opening and closing paragraphs of *Black Boy*:

> One winter morning in the long-ago, four-year-old days of my life I found myself standing before a fireplace, warming my hands over a mound of glowing coals, listening to the wind whistle past the house outside. All morning my mother had been scolding me, telling me to keep still, warning me that I must make no noise. And I was angry, fretful, and impatient. In the next room Granny lay ill and under the day and night care of a doctor and I knew that I would be punished if I did not obey. I crossed restlessly to the window and pushed back the long fluffy white curtains—which I had been forbidden to touch—and looked yearningly out into the empty street. I was dreaming of running and playing and shouting, but the vivid image of Granny's old, white, wrinkled, grim face, framed by a halo of tumbling black hair, lying upon a huge feather pillow, made me afraid.

With ever watchful eyes and bearing scars, visible and invisible, I headed North, full of a hazy notion that life could be lived with dignity, that the personalities of others should not be violated, that men should be able to confront other men without fear or shame, and that if men were lucky in their living on earth they might win some redeeming meaning for their having struggled and suffered here beneath the stars.

The young man going north, scarred and watchful, in search of redemption by meaning, has remarkably little connection with the four-year-old boy, impatient for the dream of running, playing, and shouting. Wright's purpose is to explain his fall from impulse into care, and his inevitable explanation will be social and historical. Yet much that he loses is to his version of the family romance, as he himself describes it, and some of what vanishes from him can be ascribed, retrospectively, to a purely personal failure; in him the child was not the father of the man.

What survives best in *Black Boy*, for me, is Wright's gentle account of his human rebirth as a writer. At eighteen, reading Mencken, he learns audacity, the agonistic use of language, and an aggressive passion for study comes upon him. After reading Sinclair Lewis's *Main Street*, he is found by the inevitable precursor in Theodore Dreiser:

> "That's deep stuff you're reading, boy."
> "I'm just killing time, sir."
> "You'll addle your brains if you don't watch out."

I read Dreiser's *Jennie Gerhardt* and *Sister Carrie* and they revived in me a vivid sense of my mother's suffering; I was overwhelmed. I grew silent, wondering about the life around me. It would have been impossible for me to have told anyone what I derived from these novels, for it was nothing less than a sense of life itself. All my life had shaped me for the realism, the naturalism of the modern novel, and I could not read enough of them.

Steeped in new moods and ideas, I bought a ream of paper and tried to write; but nothing would come, or what did come was flat beyond telling. I discovered that more than desire and feeling were necessary to write and I dropped the idea. Yet I still wondered how it was possible to know people sufficiently to write about them? Could I ever learn about life and people? To me, with my vast ignorance, my Jim Crow station in life, it seemed a task impossible of achievement. I now knew what being a Negro meant. I could endure the hunger. I had learned to live with hate. But to feel that there were feelings denied me, that the very breath of life was beyond my reach, that more than anything else hurt, wounded me. I had a new hunger.

Dreiser's taut visions of suffering women renew in Wright his own memories of his mother's travails and make him one of those authors for whom the purpose of the poem (to cite Wallace Stevens) is the mother's face. There is an Oedipal violence in Wright that sorts strangely with his attempt to persuade us, and himself, that all violence is socially overdetermined. *Black Boy*, even now, performs an ethical function for us by serving as a social testament, as Wright intended it to do. We can hope that someday the book will be available to us as a purely individual treatment and then may read very differently.

Biographical Sketch

The compelling biographical question raised by Richard Wright's life is why it did not follow a course similar to that of his character Bigger Thomas from *Native Son*. At the end of his completed autobiography, Wright finds himself alone in his rented Chicago room, having just returned from a May Day parade in which he had planned to march with his union as part of the Communist Party of America. Citing some earlier act of "disloyalty," a white communist member has ordered him out of the parade, and a black communist friend no longer supports his right to be there. Wright is left feeling both isolated and alienated but not unchanged. "I had outgrown my childhood," he explains to himself and his readers. (*Black Boy* [*American Hunger*] 1993, 450). The marchers, he concludes, are blind; and only further life experience will teach them the maturity that Wright feels he has already achieved.

Back in his room, he expresses his anger and frustration through words of reflection. He realizes that the ideals of the Communist Party are wrong sighted and will, like all other efforts to solve human problems, fail. More ominously, he realizes that "[his] country had shown [him] no examples of how to live a human life [and that he was left now] full of a hunger for a new way to live" (452). It was 1936, and on the radio in his room he hears news that foretells the coming of World War II. He thinks: "Yes, the whites were as miserable as their black victims. . . . If this country can't find its way to a human path . . . then all of us, black as well as white, are going down the same drain" (453).

What is notable about these reflections is that Wright does not endorse violence as an answer, nor does he despair or turn away from what he understands as an approaching national tragedy. His way, he concludes, will use words as weapons. There were many who had grown up in the same oppressive situations who would not have chosen to seek out the power of words. Wright ended his autobiography with these thoughts:

I wanted to try to build a bridge of words between me and that world outside, that world which was so distant and elusive that it seemed unreal. I would hurl words into this darkness and wait for an echo, and if an echo sounded, no matter how faintly, I would send other words to tell, to march, to fight, to create a sense of the hunger for life that gnaws in us all, to keep alive in our hearts a sense of the inexpressibly human. (453)

The main source of information about Wright's life and developing sensibilities is his own autobiography, first published in 1945 as *Black Boy: A Record of Childhood and Youth*, and later, in 1977, in a significantly expanded version called *American Hunger*. Although some critics and later biographers found inaccuracies and inconsistencies in parts of *Black Boy*, most readers look to that work first for the essential facts of Wright's early life.

Both sets of Wright's grandparents had been slaves, and the family traced its roots to Mississippi, the state known for enacting the most reactionary and restrictive measures controlling the lives of its black citizens, all aiming to preserve a so-called "southern way of life." This preservation of tradition, in the form of racial inequality, was the aim of the organization known as the Ku Klux Klan (KKK) and other white supremacist groups; public lynchings (and the ever-present threat of lynching) were their means. Any effort on the part of black residents to call attention to the multiple injustices they endured in Mississippi carried a threat of death. As to any legal recourse, lynchings were often carried out in the approving presence of the local sheriff or law-enforcement official.

Wright was born with the help of an undertrained midwife on September 4, 1908, in an unpainted log cabin in Roxie, Mississippi, a sharecropper community of 200 people. Official birth records of black babies were not kept at the time, so none exists for Richard Nathanial Wright (named after his grandfathers), a fact that prompted him later to explain that he had "come out of nowhere."

One prominent feature of Wright's childhood was its unsettledness. Poverty was the motivating factor for the frequent moves the family made, and adjusting to different living conditions, the variable availability of food, and the rules of other family members were among the most vivid of young Wright's memories. Also prominent in his recollections was an awareness of the existence of nature just outside his doorstep; childhood glimpses and views of distant fields may have unconsciously stirred him in later years to seek realities beyond the enclosing boundaries that governed parts of his young life.

In two of the family moves, Wright famously initiates two unforgettable acts of violent destruction, both described in the first pages of *Black Boy*. The first was his apparently accidentally setting fire to the house of his maternal grandparents. Restless, rebellious, and feeling too restricted because he was not allowed to make any sound that would disturb his ailing grandmother, Wright ignites a few broom straws and then, excited by his power and undeterred by his younger brother's objections, he sets the curtains on fire. The flames quickly spread to the walls and ceilings of the house. No one perishes, but when he is discovered in his hiding place—inexplicably under the burning house—Wright is punished by his mother with a whipping so severe a doctor is summoned who warns that the four-year-old had come close to losing his life.

The second incident Wright recounts is as disturbing as the first but perhaps less inexplicable. In a conscious act of rebellion, Wright deliberately literalizes his father's annoyed suggestion that the kitten meowing outside his room be killed. Wright promptly and ruthlessly ties a rope around the animal and, in effect, lynches it. About this episode Wright remembers more vividly having to bury the cat in the dark, as ordered by his mother, than acknowledging the suffering he caused an innocent animal. It is clear from the beginning that the profound anger and frustration Wright experienced under the influence of hunger, fearfulness, and all manner of deprivation his family faced, manifested themselves in explosive and violent acts. Despite their extremity, Wright still gleans important lessons from his destructive behaviors. He recalls the experience with the kitten as one that taught him that words can have multiple meanings, both metaphorical and literal. The lesson about words lasted a lifetime.

In 1914, the family moved to Memphis by steamboat, a highly anticipated adventure that ended in disappointment because the boat was small and modest in design. When Wright's father deserts the family, choosing to live with another woman, long periods of poverty and struggle prevail. Wright and his brother are even placed briefly in an orphanage when their mother falls ill. Another move to live with relatives in Arkansas brings Wright face to face with his first personal instance of racial terror when white men murder his uncle, Silas Hoskins, because they want to take over his successful liquor business. Fearing for its own safety, the family flees to another part of Arkansas.

This was not the only act of racial violence that would touch Wright's life. A man Wright knew who had entered into a relationship with a white woman was castrated, tortured, and murdered. Like the murdered uncle, the young man was victimized because he had crossed a boundary created by whites. Wright was not one to cower helplessly before such threats, but the message from these events and hundreds of others was clear: Black people could not aspire to any measure of success, equality, or social change without fear of the worst kind of reprisal.

The frequent moves the family made meant sporadic schooling for Wright, but his curiosity and interest in reading continued unabated, and he graduated in 1925 from a Jackson, Mississippi, junior high school as valedictorian of his class. In a gesture Wright presented as having been a noble act of rebellion, he refused to read the speech prepared for him by the principal, drafting his own and presenting it despite warnings not to. According to Michel Fabre, a biographer of Wright, this episode apparently had a more benign explanation and is one instance of the "fictionalized" aspects of Wright's autobiography.

Throughout these years, Wright and his family received consistent support from other family members—mainly in being taken in when too poor to pay rent—but Wright was also gradually pulling away from family influences. He never quite gives credit to the members of his extended family who frequently and often swiftly came to his family's aid.

A major influence on Wright was his discovery of H.L. Mencken through a newspaper editorial denouncing the iconoclastic cultural critic. Too poor to buy Mencken's books, he hatched a scheme—another rebellious act—to have a white library patron take out the books for him. Mencken's writings opened a new world to Wright; he was excited to read words that debunked white hypocrisy and the brutal backwardness of the South. He was even more excited to learn of Mencken's use of words as "weapons." This discovery led Wright to a program of self-education that included reading other American writers such as Sinclair Lewis and Theodore Dreiser and European writers such as Feodor Dostoevsky and Friedrich Nietzsche. Wright's notion of himself as a writer and cultural critic was solidifying, and he was finally able to save enough money to leave Memphis and move, in December 1927, to Chicago where he expected racism to be less overt and his chance for success greatly improved.

A series of odd jobs and thwarted attempts at publishing characterized Wright's first years in Chicago. He lost out on a chance for a job with the U.S. Postal Service for being found "unfit" because of malnutrition, but he made an effort to put on weight and passed a subsequent test. The 1929 stock market crash only deepened Wright's poverty, and he sought relief in the form of two Works Progress Administration (WPA) jobs with the Federal Negro Theatre and the Illinois Writers Project.

Becoming involved with the John Reed Club and the American Communist Party was another major point in Wright's life. When he joined the John Reed Club (memorably documented in the film *Reds*), Wright found a sympathetic and mainly white audience for his writing, especially his poetry centering on revolutionary themes. He began to read *New Masses* and *International Literature*, both connected to the International League of Revolutionary Writers. The leftist views of these organizations spoke to Wright's experiences with labor injustices and racial discrimination and brutality. Fighting for the rights of black Americans had become major issues for John Reed and the American communists, and Wright's work was published by both groups. In a short period of time, Wright had established himself as a notable writer and intellectual of the left. In 1937, however, he broke ranks with the John Reed Club over the issue of freedom for and the control of writers, and he moved to New York City to become the Harlem editor of the *Daily Worker*, a communist newspaper. Before leaving Chicago, Wright had taken a job working with a group of street kids, unemployed youth he described as "candidates for the clinics, morgues, prisons, reformatories, and the electric chair" (*Black Boy* 401). His experience with these young people was the inspiration for his novel *Native Son*.

Life in New York was full of activity: meeting other writers such as Ralph Ellison and Langston Hughes; submitting and publishing essays, articles, poems, and short stories; and—for writing "The Ethics of Living Jim Crow"—finding himself entangled in the much publicized hunt for communists and communist sympathizers initiated by Senator Joseph McCarthy's House Committee on Un-American Activities.

In 1939, Wright married Dhima Rose Meadman, with Ralph Ellison serving as best man, but the marriage soon collapsed, and a year later he married Ellen Poplar, a white woman whose parents objected to the racially mixed marriage. During this time of multiple marriages, *Native Son* was published in 1940 and became a Book-of-the-Month-Club selection. Wright and Ellen also had two daughters—Julia in 1942 and Rachel in 1949.

In 1941, the NAACP awarded Wright the prestigious Springarn Medal to recognize the black American with the most notable achievements of the year. Orson Welles, having completed *Citizen Kane*, became the director of the stage version of *Native Son*. Paul Robeson sang Wright's blues song "King Joe" with the Count Basie orchestra. Among other accomplishments, Wright published *12 Million Black Voices: A Folk History of the Negro in the United States*.

During World War II, Wright reversed his initial opposition to U.S. involvement, but as the sole provider for his family he was not drafted. He had already broken ranks with the Communist Party because its focus had turned toward the war against fascism and away from the racial issues plaguing the United States. The Federal Bureau of Investigation took up where Joseph McCarthy had left off, continuing to treat Wright as a suspicious person. *Black Boy* (1945) was the new target. Wright had tried to publish his entire autobiography—titled *American Hunger*—but he released a shorter version because the Book-of-the-Month Club would not promote the second part. Wright also made public his separation from the Communist Party by writing an essay, "I Tried to Be a Communist," printed in *The Atlantic Monthly* in 1944. In response to widespread riots in Harlem, Wright helped to organize the Citizens' Emergency Conference for Interracial Unity.

Starting in the mid-1940s, Wright's life became more international in focus. In 1946, he met the French existentialist writer Jean-Paul Sartre in New York and was invited to visit France. When a passport request was denied, he was aided by French anthropologist and cultural attaché Claude Lévi-Strauss, who was in a position to get an official invitation from the French government. With his family, he moved to France, lived mainly in Paris, and counted among his associates many French intellectuals and existentialists, including, in addition to Sartre, Simone de Beauvoir and André Gide and American expatriate Gertrude Stein. He quickly became identified with the African-American community in France, which led eventually to his association with and support of African movements for liberation and equality and correspondence with the revolutionary writer Frantz Fanon. In 1953, Wright traveled to the Gold Coast, a part of Africa now known as Ghana, that was in the throes of successfully freeing itself from British rule. His book on Africa—*Black Power: A Record of Reactions in a Land of Pathos*—was published in 1954. Other international and political activities in this period included his becoming president of the Franco-American Fellowship, which publicized racial discrimination practiced by American companies in France; his association with the proindependence Convention People's Party; surviving harassment from the U.S.

Department of State and the FBI; attending the Conference of Non-aligned Nations in Bandung, Indonesia; helping to found the American Society for African culture; publishing *White Man, Listen!*; and lecturing in Sweden, Norway, and Denmark on cultural freedom issues.

Toward the end of his life, Wright suffered from anxieties about money and his publishing career, continuing interference in his activities by the FBI, and ill health. His mother died in 1959, a year before her son. Wright maintained a wide circle of admirers from the United States and around the world and was attended to by many friends late in life. Despite a painful falling out with James Baldwin earlier in his career, Wright continued his encouragement and action on behalf of many younger writers. While recovering from a bout of dysentery he was inspired by a South African poet to experiment with the haiku form of poetry, eventually producing more than 4,000. A lingering illness brought him under the care of Victor Schwartzman, a specialist in intestinal disorders, who admired Wright's work and charged nothing for his services. Wright was given frequent doses of bismuth salts, a common treatment at the time; however, this practice was discontinued after it was later shown to cause severe liver damage. When he died from a heart attack on November 28, 1960, at the Eugene Gibez Clinic, some family members and friends felt his death had come prematurely because of the treatment. Wright's cremated remains were buried along with a copy of *Black Boy* at the Père-Lachaise Cemetery on December 5, 1960. The span of Wright's life was relatively brief; he lived only 52 years. In that time, however, he created out of very unpromising raw materials a life of literary and cultural distinction.

The Story Behind the Story

The publishing history of Richard Wright's autobiography is unusual: It exists now in two separate editions, and several editorial changes between 1944 and 1991 led to its being published in three different versions. It first appeared in 1945 as *Black Boy: A Record of Childhood and Youth*. The much longer original version, titled *American Hunger*, had been sent for review to the Book-of-the-Month Club editors by the publisher HarperCollins with the hope that its selection would increase publicity and sales. The club's review board found the second half of the manuscript—"The Horror and The Glory"— "unacceptable" because it was too critical of the United States, in general, and too specific in its descriptions of northern racism. One woman in particular, the New Englander Dorothy Canfield Fisher, who thought of herself as a humanitarian and unprejudiced liberal, tried to persuade Wright that all the northerners who had tried to help the "Negro cause" would be offended if Wright failed to acknowledge their efforts with his pessimistic and critical outlook. She wrote to him:

> To receive in the closing pages of your book, one word of recognition for this aspiration, if it were possible for you to give such recognition honestly, would hearten all who believe in American ideals. (quoted in Hazel Rowley's *Richard Wright*, 288)

Reluctantly, Wright made a few small changes but not enough to get the club's full approval, and *American Hunger* was changed to *Black Boy* with the volume ending at the point when Wright is leaving the South heading to Chicago and the North. Wright also permitted a statement on the dust jacket urging people to patriotically support the United States in the war effort by buying war bonds, but he did not repudiate his own harsh opinions. In a letter sent to Canfield Fisher while the disputed editorial content was being debated, he wrote: "I do not think that Negroes will be treated any better in this country until whites themselves realize that there is something dead wrong with the American way of life" (Rowley, 289).

HarperCollins promised to publish the rest of the work as Wright had originally wanted, and it did but not until 1977, after the author's death and in the form of page proofs only. Titled *American Hunger*, it covered Wright's experiences in Chicago. In 1991, the Library of America published *Richard Wright: Later Works*, which included both original sections— "Southern Nights" and "The Horror and the Glory"—along with a later work, *The Outsider*. Readers of Wright would not get the whole story, as Wright had envisioned it, until HarperCollins published *Black Boy (American Hunger): A Record of Childhood and Youth* in 1993 with an introduction by Jerry W. Ward Jr. Notwithstanding the various efforts to get the separate texts combined and published in a single volume, Wright scholars generally agree that the shorter version—the first 14 chapters, the section originally called "Southern Nights"—is the superior portion. That version is the one discussed in the Summary and Analysis section (p. 29).

Wright's reputation had already been established with the publication of *Native Son* in 1940, so an enthusiastic readership was ready to appreciate another work. The critical and popular reception of the book was mainly positive. *Black Boy* was on the *New York Times* bestseller list for three months and had such an influence on other black writers that a small circle became known as "the Wright School" of African-American writing. Not everyone was enthusiastic in their opinions and reviews, however. One rejection of the work was so extreme as to be almost amusing. When *Black Boy* came out as a Book-of-the-Month Club selection, a senator from Mississippi, Theodore Gilman Bilbo, made it his task to condemn the book in a speech on the floor of the U.S. Senate:

It [*Black Boy*] is a damnable lie from beginning to end. It is practically all fiction. There is just enough truth to enable him to build his fabulous lies about his experiences in the South. . . . It is the dirtiest, filthiest, lousiest, most obscene piece of writing that I have ever seen in print. . . .

But it comes from a Negro and you can't expect anything better from a person of this type. (From *Proceedings and Debates of the 70th Congress:* First Session, vol. 91, no. 218, June 27, 1945; quoted in Michel Fabre, *The Unfinished Quest of Richard Wright*, 282)

Included in the notes provided by biographer Michel Fabre are remarks Wright made in reaction to Bilbo. In a letter to a friend, he wrote: "Did you see what Bilbo (THE MAN!) said about me in the U. S. Senate? Seems that the folks in Miss. are learning that a Black Boy once lived there. But I think *Black Boy* will be read when Bilbo is dead and his name forgotten" (quoted in Fabre, 585).

More substantial criticism came from W.E.B. Du Bois who questioned whether the obviously fictionalized aspects of the autobiography also undermined the authenticity of the work. Du Bois also criticized—as did many other commentators— the unwillingness and/or inability of Wright to find redeeming qualities about other black people, as if no one but the author was capable of rising to his level of action and reflection. "Overdrawn" and "not representative" were other common complaints. A more recent and related observation was made by the scholar and historian Henry Louis Gates Jr., who wrote in *The Signifying Monkey* (1988) that "[in *Black Boy*] Wright's humanity is achieved only at the expense of his fellow blacks, pitiful victims of the pathology of slavery and racial segregation who surround and suffocate him" (182). Commentator Isidor Schneider, writing in the April 3, 1945, *New Masses*, was able to separate Wright's "distortions" from the work as "a document of the psychological patterns of race tension" which he praised for being "unique, powerful, and of considerable importance" (John M. Reilly, ed. *Richard Wright: The Critical Reception*, 149). The noted literary and cultural critic Lionel Trilling gave Wright high praise for presenting with unforgettable force the "spiritual imprisonment" and "personal humiliation" endured by black people in the South and the North—a "tragic situation," he called it in his review for *The Nation* on April 7, 1945, one for which "the full amount of anger that would be appropriate . . . alone would surely have the effect of quite destroying the person who felt it" (article reprinted in Reilly, 152).

The dominant theme in the general praise surrounding *Black Boy* was its success at exposing a disturbing truth about American society that could be addressed only if fully acknowledged. Jerry W. Ward Jr. was one of those whose appreciation of Wright's accomplishment was especially keen. In his introduction to *Black Boy* (1993), Ward cites the importance of Wright's implicit observation that "the Promised Land was nowhere in America" (*Black Boy* xii). Wright succeeded in demythologizing the American Dream and made it clear that the noble, democratic, and idealistic assurances of life, liberty, and the pursuit of happiness—assurances ostensibly held out for all citizens—are unattainable by the minority populations for whom "death, unfreedom, and the flight from despair" are the more likely realities. Ward concludes his reading of the complete autobiography with a comment implicitly but unmistakably linking Wright with John F. Kennedy:

> In [Wright's] humanistic affirmation [at the end] is a foreshadowing of the charge that would come several decades later to ask not what our country could do for us, but rather what we might do for our country. (xxi)

Understanding the political and social background informing *Black Boy* requires familiarity with the realities of life under the Jim Crow laws. These dictates—a quasilegal system that included traditional sanctions—enforced a complete segregation of activities for blacks and whites. This ideology and system of control was upheld and expanded by members of the KKK. The segregation laws affected all black citizens. In addition to segregated schools, there were "black" and "white-only" sections in most public buildings, restrooms, waiting rooms, restaurants, parks, theaters, and churches. The black residential sections in towns and communities were historically inferior: The roads were unpaved, trash was infrequently collected, police protection was nonexistent, and not only were black schools underfunded and poorly maintained, in most communities there were no high schools for black students.

The reign of Jim Crow was particularly harsh in Mississippi and particularly oppressive during the decades when Wright was growing up there. Understood for what it was—a system of education designed to teach black people about their inferiority and the futility of attempting to create change or to act as if they were equals—one could say that *Black Boy* emerges as resounding proof that Richard Wright did not learn, absorb, or internalize the lessons in humiliation and intimidation that the Jim Crow system was meant to promote. Some of the criticism the book received—mainly about it not being a conventional autobiography—may be resolved by understanding that Wright was writing explicitly to represent not only himself but also the "voiceless Negro boys" caught in the same psychological and cultural prison.

List of Characters

Richard Wright is an author and activist whose life, work, and historical background are documented in biographies and works of literary criticism. Richard is the name most commonly invoked when imparting the thoughts and sensibilities attributed to the author as he remembers and records his experiences growing up. Dick, a nickname for Richard, is sometimes (though infrequently) used by Wright's friends in conversation.

Nathaniel Wright, Richard's father, grew up more impoverished than his sons, and he had no hopes of finding a job that would sustain a family. His consciousness developed completely under the conditions imposed by segregation, and the reality of slavery was as near as his own parents' recent memories. Nathan Wright moved his family twice, once to his wife's parents' house and once to Memphis. The disturbing scene in which Richard strangles the kitten occurs when he decides to take literally his father's angry command to kill it, despite knowing that his father meant the words figuratively. The episode is important for the experience it provides Richard with the power of words and the distortion of meaning. The importance of Nathan in Richard's life is mainly his absence; he deserted the family for another woman, and, on the two occasions Richard describes being with his father, his father seems oblivious to his son's needs. Richard carries through his life far more contempt for his father than pity.

Ella Wilson Wright, Richard's mother, was born to ex-slaves who managed to provide her with enough education so that she became a schoolteacher, instructing the children of sharecroppers, near Natchez, Mississippi. Ella married Nathan in 1908, and they made their first home in nearby Roxie, where Richard and his brother were born. Ella's life became a ceaseless struggle after Nathan deserted the family; she took one low-paying job after another and at one point was so desperate she put both sons temporarily in an orphanage. Although Ella has aspirations for her sons, her support for them decreases as she becomes weary from overwork and ill health. Her illness brings about the first separation of the family. Poverty and racism prevent Ella from receiving the medical care she needs, and, in 1923, she has her third stroke, which paralyzes her and results in the boys being placed in separate homes. Richard is always aware of his mother's prolonged and unrelieved suffering. Watching her through the years inspires his lifelong desire to turn senseless suffering into something meaningful. Ella is an ally during Richard's early years, and Wright remained loyal and attentive to her throughout his life. She is responsible for introducing her son to the pleasures of reading and for teaching him to pay attention to the meaning of words. She died one year before he did, in 1959.

Leon Wright, Richard's younger brother by two years, figures little in Richard's story of growing up. After their mother's stroke, Leon goes to live with his Aunt Maggie, which separated the brothers for several years.

Margaret Wilson (Granny), Richard's maternal grandmother and a former slave, is fiercely and rigidly pious, quick to punish, and utterly unsympathetic to her grandson's zeal for reading. Wright describes her as being "as nearly white as a Negro can get without being white, which means that she was white" (48). He learns later that she has "white" blood from Scotch and Irish "infusions." Granny converted from Methodism to become a Seventh Day Adventist and imposed a nearly impossible religious regimen on her family members that involved dietary restrictions, daylong prayers, ascetic practices, Bible reading, prohibitions of most other reading materials, and working on the Sabbath (Saturday in the Seventh Day Adventist Church). Granny is the rock of the family, however, despite the harsh way of life she imposes on her family. She was present in Richard's life on and off for years and seemed always to be nearby when some transgression called for a whipping. Everything Richard wanted to read or write Granny condemned and forbade as "the Devil's work," assuring him on many occasions that his fate for being a sinner would be to spend eternity in the burning lakes of Hell. Despite Richard's ongoing conflicts with Granny, however, he remained respectful of her and appreciated the rare moments when she found reason to praise him. At the height of the family chaos brought on by his mother's illness, Richard's first thought is how he can get Granny to come to the rescue.

Richard Wilson, Wright's maternal grandfather, joined the Navy and fought on the Union side in the Civil War. The source of his longstanding bitterness about white people is revealed at the end of *Black Boy*. His resentment was so extreme that Richard had assumed it was the reason his grandfather never spoke about white people. The full explanation comes to light just as the old man is dying and concerns his great consternation over not receiving his pension from the government because his name had been misspelled on the original records. In addition, the records that would have contained his name at the time of enlistment no longer existed. Despite many letters written to different offices of the government—first in explanation and then in protest—no reply ever came, and the family suffered financially as a result. As might be expected in one who is remembered for his bitterness, Richard recalls that his grandfather had two facial "oddities": when angry, he hissed and bared his teeth.

Addie Wilson was Richard's youngest aunt and the one toward whom he experienced the greatest acrimony. She was the only teacher at the Seventh Day Adventist school, which she and Granny forced Richard to attend instead of the public school, and she was particularly harsh with her nephew. After a dispute in the classroom over some walnut pieces spilled on the floor (Richard was not responsible), Richard finds her at home ready to carry through with her threatened punishment. The two get into a dangerous physical fight, with Richard holding a knife to defend himself against what he knows with certainty is a false charge. This daring refusal to confess to a false charge and his subsequent willingness to defend himself is the first time Richard stands up to a figure of authority.

Thomas Wilson, another of Richard's uncles, lives in Granny's Jackson house and disapproves of Richard during the two years they live there together. Frequent arguments flare up between uncle and nephew, including the incident when Richard uses razors to fend off his uncle's threatened physical assault. When Richard overhears his uncle warning his daughter, Maggie, not to spend time with her cousin, he suddenly realizes that he has never been allowed to play alone with her. This unjustified prejudice enrages Richard. In a later incident, Uncle Tom unsuccessfully counsels Richard to submit to the principal's wishes about the valedictorian speech, which Richard sees as an example of black capitulation to white authority—a predilection in many black southerners that he detested.

Maggie Wilson Hoskins is Richard's aunt. When Richard's father deserts his family in 1916, Richard, his mother, and brother make the first of their frequent moves to live with a family member willing to take them in. They are invited to stay with Aunt Maggie and Uncle Silas who live in Elaine, Arkansas. Richard called Maggie his favorite aunt and second mother. After Maggie's husband is killed in a racial incident, she flees with the rest of her family to avoid being killed herself. Later, she takes up with a mysterious and somewhat menacing older man and one night suddenly disappears with him.

Silas Hoskins is the husband of Wright's Aunt Maggie. When Richard's family moves in with them in 1916, Silas takes responsibility for teaching Richard about life in a way that his biological father never did. Silas was the first man Richard associated with feeling security and comfort. The time that Silas spent residing with the couple was also the first time the family had enough food. The sudden disappearance and murder of Silas by white racists who resent his success leaves Richard with lasting bitterness and a deep sense of deprivation.

Clark Wilson, another of Richard's uncles, was self-employed as a contracting carpenter in Greenwood, Mississippi, where Richard went to live at the age of 10 after one of his mother's illnesses. Although Clark and his wife have financial resources to provide for Richard, they are among the more stern members of the family, and Richard feels like a stranger in their home. Life in that household becomes intolerable for Richard after he learns that a young boy, formerly a tenant, had died in the bed Richard is using. The reality of death is too close in this situation, and Richard is unable to sleep for days. Despite having enrolled his nephew in school and making other provisions, Uncle Clark agrees to the boy's pleas to be returned to his mother.

Jody Wilson, described by Wright as "a medium-sized, neat, silent mulatto girl," is Clark's wife and another of Richard's aunts (though not his favorite). She is stern and demanding, insisting during his stay that Richard speak "correct" English, demonstrate good manners, and attend church. Richard felt trapped in her presence and baffled by the code of conduct she enforced in her home.

Ella is a boarder who is evicted from the household by Granny when she is discovered reading *Bluebird and His Seven Wives* to young Richard. Her importance in introducing him to the seductive appeal of the written word is conveyed by Richard's own acknowledgment. He calls the moment a "turning point" in his life.

Griggs is a classmate of Richard's in ninth grade who also gives a speech at graduation but accepts without resistance the one written for him by the principal. Later, Griggs gets Richard a job with Mr. Crane at the optical shop but not before offering his cautionary advice about the "safe" way for blacks to behave around whites.

Ned Greenley is one of Richard's classmates who delivers the appalling news of his brother's kidnapping, torture, and murder by a white gang as punishment for being with a white prostitute.

Mr. Crane, a northern entrepreneur, not only offers Richard a job in his optical factory but is kind and solicitous and suggests he might be able to train Richard for a higher-paying and more professional position. When Richard becomes too scared to work in the factory, Crane gives him extra money and supports his decision to seek a better life in the North.

Pease and **Reynolds** are employees in Crane's optical factory who have neither the decency not the enlightened views about race that their boss, Mr. Crane, possesses. They quickly develop a homicidal resentment toward Richard. They trick him into having to admit to being a liar or an "uppity" black—either of which, according to their system of justice, deserves punishment by death. Their combined presence in the factory is too menacing for Richard, and, because of them, he leaves the job, an action that plunges him into a period of despair and defeat.

Summary and Analysis

Chapter one of *Black Boy* begins explosively. Young Richard Wright—only four years old at the time—sets fire to his grandmother's house. In this first scene, he recalls how restrained he was feeling in a female-dominated household in which his grandmother, in her sickbed, needed silence and his mother demanded it accordingly. His understandable frustration is initially expressed in a benign way. He rebels against not being allowed to touch the long, fluffy, white curtains in the windows. Then, though seemingly accidental, his anger finds a destructive form, as he sets fire first to a few straws from a broom and then to the curtains. As flames shoot up the walls and engulf the house, Richard flees the burning house and hides beneath it. Screams and other sounds of panic ensue. Despite hearing his name called by his frantic parents, he does not move, a potential sign of a greater fear of punishment than of perishing under a burning house. This psychological state of impatience, anger, frustration, and terror characterize much of Richard's life and develop into a spirit of defiance that is frequently extreme to the point of irrational. This feeling of resistance is Richard's first weapon.

Richard's fear of punishment is as severe as the punishment itself; his mother ("You almost scared us to death") strips a tree limb to make a whip and beats him to a point that the summoned doctor judges to have been near death. Later, Richard receives another punishment, again administered by his mother, this time for an act of gratuitous cruelty. He strangles a stray kitten whose cries have been keeping his father awake. Richard justifies his act and expresses his hatred of his father by deliberately literalizing his father's angry words—"Kill that damn thing! Do anything, but get it away from here!"—even though Richard knows his father was speaking figuratively. The string of punishments continues with Richard's mother honing her son's sense of guilt and ordering him to bury the "poor kitten" in the dark. Uttering the phrases of forgiveness that are part of the mother's punishment, Richard experiences a brief moment of empathy as he imagines himself gasping for breath as he had earlier observed the kitten doing.

These early scenes offer microcosmic views of the Deep South as experienced by a black boy growing up there. Between the two destructive and punishment-tinged episodes Wright relates in the opening of the work, a sense of pastoral calm and the pervasive beauty of nature emerges. In Wright's adult language, he recalls memories of sights and experiences based in natural settings. These impressions range from aesthetic and comforting (the "sensuality" of the dew on his skin, the "melancholy scent" of burning hickory wood, the "aching glory" of gold and purple clouds) to mentally stimulating ("the vague sense of the infinite" inspired by the sight of the Mississippi River, the "yearning for identification" at seeing an ant following its mysterious journey). Wright's recollections of his world also extend to images of fear and signs of mortality, the "tortured . . . blue-pink crawfish" and the just-killed chicken still thrashing about the yard. These scenes embedded in his memory inform his life and the narrative of *Black Boy* and at critical times in the ensuing years provide insight, motivation, or comfort.

Richard's family seems always to be moving, dogged by their poverty. The first move is to Memphis via a ride on the *Kate Adams*, a "dingy" ferryboat that the excited young boy imagines—with the help of his mother's description—as a glamorous cruise ship. Disappointment is another recurring emotion or reaction that colors Richard's early years. His father's comforting words—a rare instance of paternal affection—plus his own imaginative resources work to make the actual journey more exciting, with visits to the boat's engine room and the sight of the other passengers gambling and drinking on deck.

Hunger is also a prevalent theme—deep "biological hunger" that worsens after the father deserts the family. For Richard, the lack of nourishment becomes fused with deprivation of all kinds and with his unceasing hatred of his father. There are other hazards attached to hunger that Richard must contend with. One is his mother's insistence that he take the little money she earns to the grocery store to buy food. When he is beaten and robbed by a gang of street thieves three times, his mother sends him out once again to learn a survival tool critical in his world—to be able to fend for himself. With daring borne of rage and fierce hunger, he successfully beats back the gang. "That night I won the right to the streets of Memphis" (25). Another drawback of the family's enduring poverty was further dislocation, as the boys were temporarily placed in an orphanage, an extreme action deemed necessary by their desperate mother who was consistently earning too little money to support them.

Still other threats and hazards await the young boy. Out on the streets, Richard gets caught up in a gang of drinkers who frequent a bar and for their own unthinking entertainment force the unknowing six-year-old to get drunk and to relay salacious language to women in the bar. Later, he unknowingly uses one of the phrases in front of his rigidly righteous grandmother and receives for his innocent lapse another ferocious beating along with threats of damnation.

Two fortuitous events then conspire to alter the boy's prospects and worldview: Richard's mother, a woman who had worked as a schoolteacher, teaches her son how to read and how to decipher the meaning of words; then, a kind man who delivers coal to their house teaches him how to count to 100. These experiences open up new perspectives and possibilities for Richard and give him confidence in skills other than those he uses to defend himself on the street.

Formal education for Richard is sporadic; he begins late at Howard Institute. Religion becomes a dominant part of his life with attendance at his mother's church. His first encounter with a person of religious authority happens at a Sunday dinner during which the invited minister eats nearly every piece of chicken on the platter, certainly more than his share. Richard, denied a serving until he finishes his soup, watches carefully as piece after piece of chicken disappears until his rising fury prevents him from eating and, in the end, he gets no chicken at all. From that time on, Richard's associations with religion are negative. The few appealing connotations he retains—the emotional warmth of the hymns, for example—are short lived.

A tense and sad scene occurs near the end of the chapter when Richard has an unpleasant visit with his father "and a strange woman"; even when the father promises him food and a nickel if he stays with them, Richard unhesitatingly rejects the offers and leaves with his mother.

Father and son remain "forever strangers" from that point on. Wright concludes the chapter with a scene occurring a quarter century later, when Richard sees his father again. Looking disdainfully at the man, now a poor sharecropper, standing with a hoe in a muddy Mississippi field, the author writes: "I was overwhelmed to realize that he could never understand me or the scalding experiences that had swept me beyond his life and into an area of living that he could never know" (42). Richard feels no kinship to his father and only the barest of sympathies. There is a sense in which this all-but-complete rejection of both his father and the pastoral way of life could be construed as a limitation or a shortsighted generalization on Wright's part. He could see no possibility for dignity or satisfaction derived from a life on the land; it was a harsh judgment that could not have endeared him to the many individuals for whom it was the only way to survive. For Wright, his father's life is seen as a failure of both effort and imagination:

> From far beyond the horizons that bound this bleak plantation there had come to me through my living that my father was a black peasant who had gone to the city seeking life, but who had failed in the city; a black peasant whose life had been hopelessly snarled in the city, and who had at last fled the city—the same city which had lifted me in its burning arms and borne me toward alien and undreamed-of shores of knowing. (43)

Of this passage, Wright scholar Robert B. Stepto notes the themes of the "ascent" and the "quest" that, along with rejection of the father, form an underlying structure for the story:

> With these unrelenting words, Wright's persona does not so much slay his father as bury him alive. . . . The race

has been run, and the plantation-bounding horizons that entomb the beaten man do not touch let alone encompass or intersect, the "area of living" to which the victor has ascended.'. . . [The] city, a new and far more hopeful social structure erected upon what had been the site of departure for father and son alike, evolves and assumes an aggressive posture in the narrative's machinery, in triangular competition with the oppressing domestic interior and the ambiguous but unsnaring out-of-doors. Once the particular attractions of urban life for a truly questing figure are thus established, Wright's persona's flight to larger, grander, and hopefully more promising urban situations (such as Chicago) seems not just likely, but inevitable. (Stepto, "Literacy and Ascent: Richard Wright's *Black Boy*" from *From Behind the Veil: A Study of Afro-American Narrative*, University of Illinois Press, 1979: pp. 147–56. Reprinted in *Richard Wright's "Black Boy" (American Hunger): A Casebook*. Oxford University Press, 2003.)

In **chapter two,** the author again distances himself from the other blacks who make up his family and community. When Richard learns of the family's next move—this time to his mother's sister's residence in Arkansas—he has no thoughts for any of the playmates he is leaving behind: "As I shook the dingy palms [of his friends] extended to me I kept my eyes averted, not wanting to look again into faces that hurt me because they had become so thoroughly associated in my feelings with hunger and fear" (45). Wright then adds this odd reflection:

[After] the habit of reflection had been borne in me, I used to mull over the strange absence of real kindness in Negroes—how unstable was our tenderness, how lacking in genuine passion we were, how void of great hope, how timid our joy, how bare our traditions, how hollow our memories, how lacking we were in those intangible sentiments that bind man to man, and how shallow was even our despair. . . . I saw that what had been taken for our emotional strength was our negative confusions, our flights, our fears, our frenzy under pressure. (45)

Many critics and readers doubt the veracity of this statement, including those who not only dispute it but are angered by its assertions. Henry Louis Gates Jr. adds one such voice of dissent when he pointed out that Wright's story of his rise to success takes place at the expense of fellow black people:

> In his autobiographies and novels, Wright evolved a curious and complex myth of origins of self and race. . . . [His] class of ideal individual black selves seems to have included only Wright. (*The Signifying Monkey* 182)

En route to Arkansas, the family stays briefly with the maternal grandmother, now living in Jackson, Mississippi. Granny has a boarder, a bright young schoolteacher, who reluctantly reads to the eager Richard the story *Bluebird and His Seven Wives*. Her reluctance proves prescient; when Granny discovers her grandson reading such "Devil stuff," she banishes the boarder, slaps Richard, and tells him he will "burn in Hell" for his transgression. Granny's gesture is counterproductive; its effect on Richard is to make him vow "that as soon as I was old enough I would buy all the novels there were and read them to feed the thirst for violence that was in me, for intrigue, for plotting, for secrecy, for bloody murders" (48). Later in the work, he follows through of the promise, acquiring and consuming all the books he can get hold of.

This and other scenes emphasize a theme of overriding importance—the necessity of acquiring literacy for any effort to make sense of the world and one's place and purpose in it. Richard has been developing a powerful relationship with words. As he watches Ella, "weeping and distraught," packing her bags to leave after Granny accuses her of "ruining" him with her books, he thinks: "The tremendous upheaval that . . . words had caused made me know that there lay back of them much more than I could figure out" (53).

At the station waiting for the train to Arkansas, Richard has his first explicit Jim Crow experience when he notices a "white" line and a "black" line at the ticket window. On the train, black and white individuals travel in separate compartments. Richard is curious; he wants to "peep" at the white people but is forbidden by his mother who offers no helpful explanations to his questions about why there are "two sets of people who lived side by side and never touched, it seemed, except in violence" (55). From his efforts to inquire, however, he does learn that Granny, who appears white, was once a slave and had "somewhere and somehow" acquired Irish, Scotch, and French ancestry. His own identity, he learns, is as a "colored person."

From hearsay only, Richard intuits that "colored people" get beaten up and killed; not till he lives with Aunt Maggie and Uncle Hoskins, however, does the meaning of racial violence become personal. Food and comfort are finally available to him, and it turns out this prosperity is possible because Uncle Hoskins runs a successful business, a saloon patronized by black people. One night Uncle Hoskins does not return from work, and Richard describes the ominous scene of Aunt Maggie standing on the porch in the evening gloom awaiting her missing husband. In horror, they all learn that a group of white men, envious and resentful of the uncle's success, has murdered him. By dawn, the entire family, fearing for their own lives, has packed its belongings in a wagon and fled. There was no public acknowledgement of the uncle's death and no service or flowers. Richard remembers: "Uncle Hoskins had simply been plucked from our midst and we, figuratively, had fallen on our faces to avoid looking into that white-hot face of terror that we knew loomed somewhere above us" (64).

The family moves back with Granny and then, as his mother tires of the "strict religious routine," moves again to make a home in West Helena in "one half of a corner house" in front of which ran a "stagnant ditch carrying sewage." With a dime apiece for lunch, Richard and his brother roam the teeming streets in search of adventures and run into people different from them, Jews in particular. They also discover a learned prejudice that they, as blacks, carry for Jews. Some adventures are unpleasant introductions to the "adult" world: Richard discovers that a shady brothel is operating on the other side of the wall, a discovery that enrages his mother who, in complaining, in turn enrages the "madam" who insists that Richard get a beating for his interference. It is the first beating that Richard escapes; his mother cannot side with the woman who runs the brothel.

A mysterious man enters the household and is soon introduced as Aunt Maggie's new partner, a new uncle for Richard and his brother. Even identified, he remains a mystery, holding a secret that Richard learns, if it is exposed, will bring violent death to them all. One night the menacing man leaves hastily, taking Maggie with him and leaving hints that he has burned down a house while a woman was still alive inside it.

Richard hears a story about a black woman whose husband has been killed by a white mob. With a courage that only crazed grief could sustain, she hides a gun in a sheet, and, after tricking the white men into letting her take her husband's body, she kills four of them in revenge. The story deeply influences Richard; he vows to show the same courage if he is caught in a similar way: "The story of the woman's deception gave form and meaning to confused defensive feelings that had long been sleeping in me" (84). He tries to describe his hatred for whites:

> Tension would set in at the mere mention of whites and a vast complex of emotions, involving the whole of my personality, would be aroused. It was as though I was continuously reacting to the threat of some natural force whose hostile behavior could not be predicted. I had never been abused by whites, but I had already become as conditioned to their existence as though I had been the victim of a thousand lynchings. (84)

The chapter ends with Richard back in school but so intimidated by his new and curious classmates that he cannot write his name on the blackboard. The transition occurs just as

World War I is concluded: Richard is released from school with the others into the riotous celebrations. Everyone looks up at the sky to watch a strange flying object. Richard is disbelieving at first but a kindly stranger lifts him onto his shoulder and says: "Boy, remember this. You're seeing man fly" (87).

In **chapter three**, Wright joins groups of boys his own age and learns that the code of peer acceptance rests on the degree of hostility expressed toward white people. He provides for his readers a few pages of dialogue exposing the mix of bravado and fearful defensiveness that was the basis of prejudice on both sides. Real boundaries separate the turf claimed by both races, and, when violated, the "battles were real and bloody."

The chapter mainly documents Wright's growing awareness of his mother's illness and the consequences for him and his brother if she were to die. Several signs indicate his mother's serious and growing physical decline, but with no money for doctor visits and possibly no doctor easily available for black patients, the boy's helplessness is underscored all the more. His brother, Leon, discovers their mother lying inert on the bed, prompting a troop of helpful neighbor women who diagnose stroke and paralysis before a doctor arrives to confirm it. His message to all assembled—that the mother's ailment is grave and will require full-time care—prompts a new and terrifying realization for Richard, the confrontation of human mortality:

Suppose Granny did not come? I tried not to think of it. She *had* to come. The utter loneliness was now terrifying. I had been suddenly thrown upon my own. Within an hour the half-friendly world that I had known had turned cold and hostile. . . . Though I was a child, I could no longer feel as a child, could no longer react as a child. The desire for play was gone and I brooded. . . . I tried not to think of a tomorrow that was neither real nor wanted, for all tomorrows held questions that I could not answer. (96–97)

The extended family once again rallies: Granny comes, along with Aunt Maggie, Aunt Cleo, Uncle Howard, Uncle Edward, and a stream of others. With maternal supervision no longer possible, the question for Richard becomes "Where was I to go?" and with whom. There are so many uncles in attendance that he does not even identify which one stands beside him in the backyard gently inquiring about his needs and wishes. Sleepwalking becomes a symptom of his distress.

In the end, Richard calculates that his best choice is with the family that lives closest to his grandmother in Jackson, so Uncle Clark and Aunt Jody agree to take him home with them while Leon goes with Aunt Maggie. Life with his new caretakers is not easy. Richard has chores to perform and is reenrolled in school where he successfully establishes himself as a boy to be respected. The discovery, however, that a boy he never knew died in the bed now assigned to him provokes fears so irrational that he cannot sleep and finally chooses—and is allowed—to go back to his mother. Uncle Clark's effort to assuage his nephew's fears—"We all must die someday. So why be afraid?"—is in vain.

Back with his mother, Richard is relieved to find her somewhat improved, but he feels no less isolated or abandoned. He fears the outcome of the operation the doctor has advised but concludes:

> A victim myself of too many hopes that had never led anywhere, I was for letting my mother remain as she was. . . . I had already begun to sense that my feelings varied too far from those of the people around me for me to blab about what I felt. (109)

The news that his mother is turned away from the hospital because it does not serve black people only increases his frustration and loneliness. She is returned home to the care of doctors who come to the house. Richard drops out of school, and illness becomes a nonnegotiable reality infecting their lives.

When Richard's mother calls him to her bedside to tell him that she wants to die and escape her pain, he responds not so much with the heart's compassion as with the mind's reflections:

My mother's suffering grew into a symbol in my mind, gathering to itself all the poverty, the ignorance, the helplessness; the painful, baffling, hunger-ridden days and hours; the restless moving, the futile seeking, the uncertainty, the fear, the dread; the meaningless pain and the endless suffering. (111)

In critical ways, his mother's suffering intensifies and extends the trajectory Richard is already on. At the age of twelve, he notes he has had only a single year of formal education but still feels educated in the ways that seem to matter most. He is able to articulate a life-sustaining conviction that "the meaning of living came only when one was struggling to wring a meaning out of meaningless suffering" (112).

Richard views these insights as having importance mainly to his own life, but he also understands their relevance to the suffering of others. His experiences—so grave for one still so young—inspire him to become a philosopher of sorts, a metaphysician, who will "drive coldly to the heart of every question" (112).

Life with Granny returns Richard in **chapter four** to the frightful world of "vast lakes of eternal fire . . . valleys of dry bones, [the] moon turning to blood" and all the wonders and horrors of the Second Coming of Christ. In church—which he must attend in exchange for being cared for by his grandmother—he briefly falls under the spell of the preacher's message but once outside in the sun, he realizes that "none of it was true and nothing would happen" (113). Hunger persists, often to such a degree that Richard is forced to flood his stomach with water for the temporary feeling of fullness it provides. A visit from Aunt Addie results in his enrollment in a religious school where he puts in a "sullen attendance." The alienating feelings he experiences in this religious school with Aunt Addie as its domineering and ultrapious teacher remind Richard of his well-earned and authentic identity gained in the saloons, roundhouses, street fights, and orphanages that have formed so much of his life to this point.

Tension between Richard and his aunt escalates in the classroom when she accuses him of dropping walnut pieces on the floor, a minor infraction for which he knows another boy is responsible. With mounting integrity, he refuses to falsely confess or to break the code of loyalty by turning in the real culprit. The dispute becomes physical and continues at home when Richard is forced to hold a knife against his aunt who becomes obsessed with enacting physical retribution on her nephew. Richard's life at home begins to feel like a battle zone where he is consistently under siege.

Despite surviving beyond his twelfth year "on a diet that would have stunted an average-sized dog," Richard emerges into adolescence and begins to experience the first promptings of lust, which he unabashedly directs toward the minister's wife. Resisting the obvious option of sending Richard to the local (and secular) public school, Richard's family contrives a plan, involving his pious classmates, to convince him of his need to be "saved." Not feeling a need to be spiritually transformed in that way, Richard arrives at a remarkably mature conclusion:

> I reasoned that if there did exist an all-wise, all-powerful God who knew the beginning and the end, who meted out justice to all, who controlled the destiny of man, this God would surely know that I doubted His existence and He would laugh at my foolish denial of Him. And if there was no God at all, then why all the commotion? I could not imagine God pausing in His guidance of unimaginably vast worlds to bother with me. (127)

Richard devises a plan to not only please and appease his grandmother but also to remove himself from the focus of God's attentions. During a service, he whispers to Granny that if he were ever to see a ghost—as Richard has learned Jacob in the Bible had done—then he would also believe in God. Inexplicably to Richard, this news makes Granny and everyone ecstatic until, confounded, Richard realizes his words have been exactly reversed in meaning, that she thought he was confessing to already having seen a ghost. Her hopes deflated after learning of her mistaken assumption, Granny returns home with Richard but not before thinking of one last way to persuade him to want to be saved. With a mix of guilt and affection for Granny, Richard agrees to pray for help, but his daily efforts become a "nuisance" that "ruin his days." In response to his frustrating and often unmanageable situation, he writes a story, a romantic one about a young Indian woman who has to die for some mysterious reason and does so with dignity, grace, and without protest. No one, including Richard, understands the story, but the gestures of making it up and then telling it remain, inexplicably, satisfying.

In **chapter five**, Granny and his aunt have given up all hope of "saving Richard" and he, in turn, declares himself liberated from the world of eternal rewards and punishments. The mundane and, in his eyes, demeaning world of chores remains, however, as Richard is forced by his relatives to wash and iron his own clothes. This failure to understand domestic chores—if not domestic life overall—as being worthy of respect dominates much of Richard's early life and signifies to some readers a failure of imagination and a lack of compassion.

Seeking to redress what he thinks of as a lopsided education—marked by too much feeling and too little knowledge—Richard returns to school for what will be a four-year stint, finally offered a chance at a real education. After establishing himself again as a respected presence in the classroom, Richard studies hard and is promoted from fifth to sixth grade—an achievement so thrilling he starts imagining himself capable of anything. He begins to miss mealtimes at home so he can continue his learning in after-school sessions, and, although again desperately hungry, he concludes: "To starve in order to learn about my environment was irrational, but so were my hungers" (140). The signs of the future writer are potentially on display, as he establishes himself as an observer of his fellow humans, noting their diversity and joining them in their various pursuits, "[tramping] with a gang into the woods, to rivers, to creeks, into the business district, to the doors of poolrooms, into the movies when we could slip in without paying, to neighborhood ball games, to brick kilns, to lumberyards, to cottonseed mills to watch men at work" (140).

Granny forbids his working on Saturdays, the Sabbath for Seventh Day Adventists, which nearly eliminates his chances for getting a job. In a stroke of luck, he secures employment nonetheless. Getting a job and the job itself both seem like small miracles to Richard, since it involves delivering newspapers that serialize Zane Grey's *Riders of the Purple Sage*. He can bring the papers home as long as he is not delivering them on Saturday, and he easily outsmarts Granny about what he is reading because she is illiterate. Reading becomes his introduction to the "modern world and vast cities" and his "gateway to the world" (142). Richard's excitement, however, is short lived; he becomes aware, through the thoughtful intervention of one of the customers on his paper route, that the particular newspaper he delivered, though said to originate in Chicago, was a major promoter of the Ku Klux Klan, a fact he has failed to discern by choosing to read the serial narratives and ignoring the rest of the newspapers' contents.

In an idle moment during a hot summer, Richard is inadvertently responsible for an accident when he instinctively and successfully ducks to escape one of Granny's face slaps and Granny's momentum causes her to fall down the porch steps. Her wrenched back keeps her in bed for six weeks, but more momentously, Aunt Addie, who had witnessed the episode, accuses Richard of trying to kill Granny. Their mutual animosity is once again rekindled. Religion, of the kind espoused and practiced in Granny's household, fails to bring about anything of positive value—certainly not for Richard, but seemingly not for Granny and Addie either. Richard concludes:

> Wherever I found religion in my life, I found strife, the attempt of one individual or group to rule another in the name of God. The naked will to power seemed always to walk in the wake of a hymn. (150)

Richard earns a flattering description as a "pretty boy from Jackson [who can] write 'n speak" when he is asked to accompany an illiterate insurance agent on his rounds into the countryside to fill in the forms for his black clients. He experiences a deserved measure of pride in being of service to people not very different from him at one time, but he continues to have an ethical "blind spot" about black people, conveyed in these remarks:

> I saw a bare, bleak pool of black life and I hated it; the people were alike, their homes were alike, and their farms were alike. (151)

The death of Richard's grandfather concludes the chapter. Richard learns of his illness the way he learns a lot of family information—through the content of morning prayers. To this point, Richard's life has been dominated by women, but with the approaching death of the grandfather, details of the elder man's life are revealed, including the fact that, after serving in the Union Army, he was never able to get the guaranteed disability pension. For some bureaucratic—and possibly political—reason, his name was improperly entered in the records. Bitterness ensues. Richard realizes he has never heard his grandfather speak of white people and surmises that he refrained because he hated them "too much to talk about them." Richard, with his chronic hunger and sense of justice, imagines a letter coming from the government announcing that his grandfather's pension request is legitimate and apologizing for the exceedingly long delay. No such letter ever comes, of course, and the man dies without compensation or official recognition.

The chapter ends with Richard making another gesture of defiance—he insists on being allowed to have a job. After the usual round of warnings from Granny, Richard prevails, and his mother, sensing the importance of his act, supports and encourages him in the face of such resistance.

In **chapter six**, Richard goes to work for a white woman who exposes her racial and psychological ignorance about human nature when she asks him whether or not he steals. He gets the job, but it is a qualified triumph because he cannot let himself work for someone who thinks moldy milk and stale bread will nourish a young boy and assumes he is deluded in wanting to become a writer. The next prospective employer assumes—again, incorrectly—that Richard can milk a cow before offering to teach him. The people who gather around the breakfast table—Richard wonders whether it is or is not a family—are an especially unruly bunch, meanspirited and rude, disdainful of the food on the table that looks to Richard like a feast. Richard is ensured for the first time in a long time that he has enough to eat. With the self-pride that comes from his developing work ethic, Richard more confidently engages the other students at school, but his schoolwork, because of his mounting responsibilities, begins to suffer.

Richard's mother, meanwhile, partially recovers her health and strength, enough to rebel against her own mother by joining the less fundamentalist Methodist Church. Richard, who attends at her urging, stays connected because of his need for company. Despite being wary of the religious manipulations of others, Richard is craftily seduced into a prayer meeting designed to bring about submission to God. Wright makes a different judgment:

> This business of saving souls had no ethics; every human relationship was shamelessly exploited. In essence, the tribe was asking us if we shared its feelings; if we refused to join the church, it was equivalent to saying no, to placing ourselves in the position of moral monsters. (170)

For love of his mother or, more accurately, to protect her from humiliation, Richard consents to be baptized, but he walks home "limp as a rag . . . [feeling nothing] except sullen anger and a crushing sense of shame" (170). He is not alone, however, in his reactions: beyond the hearing of parents and clergymen, several boys admit to also feeling nothing and to realizing that the "entire thing was a fraud."

The chapter ends with a strange and unpleasant encounter between Richard and another of the well-meaning but misguided uncles, this time Uncle Tom who has misunderstood or misheard words Richard has spoken. The confrontation winds into another barrage of curses and warnings until Richard sadly collapses within his own broken ego.

In **chapter seven**, it is 1924, and Richard goes to work at a brickyard bringing water to the workers and picking up broken bricks. The boss's dog bites him, but the boss dismisses any possibility of an infection because he believes that no dog was capable of harming or injuring a black person.

With Granny's hints that it is time for him to move out and begin a new venture in life, Richard has to face his future more realistically than ever:

> What was it that made the hate of whites for blacks so steady, seemingly so woven into the texture of things? What kind of life was possible under that hate? . . . Was I right when I resisted punishment? It was inconceivable to me that one should surrender to what seemed wrong, and most of the people I had met seemed wrong. Ought one to surrender to authority even if one believed that authority was wrong? If the answer was yes, then I knew that I would always be wrong, because I would never do it. Then how could one live in a world in which one's mind and perceptions meant nothing and authority and tradition meant everything? There were no answers. (182)

Richard persists in asking difficult questions about the best course and conduct in navigating the world around him, even when there are no easy or satisfying answers. Confronting impediments—large and small—usually causes him distress, sometimes great pain, but he persists. The same spirit of endurance animates his efforts to write his first story and see it through to publication. With the unlikely title *The Voodoo of Hell's Half-Acre*, it is published in serialized form for no compensation other than the thrill of getting his name in print and his work before potential readers, an arrangement that Richard comes to realize may not be fair but is valuable nonetheless. His success prompts disbelief from his classmates, accusations of doing the "Devil's work" from Granny, fear from his mother that writing stories is a sign of personal weakness, and condemnation of his upbringing from Aunt Addie.

Because Richard's life is cut off from the larger world, he thinks those immediately around him—whom he already deems to be of unsound judgment—are his only critics. Inexplicably an optimist, Richard entertains dreams of "going North" and becoming a successful writer:

> I had been building up in me a dream which the entire educational system of the South had been rigged to stifle. I was feeling the very thing that the state of Mississippi had spent millions of dollars to make sure I would never feel. . . . I was beginning to dream the dreams that the state had said were wrong, that the schools had said were taboo. (186–87)

Chapter eight includes an account of one of the most brutal manifestations of racism. Richard learns that the brother of a friend has been taken to the woods in a car by a gang of whites bent on teaching him a lesson about not having sexual relations with a white woman. Historical records of crimes like this inevitably include details of torture and castration that precede the final act of murder. Again, the reality of racism—in yet another gruesome form—becomes personal. The impact on Richard's mind is savage enough to "[block] the springs of thought and feeling in [him], creating a sense of distance between [him] and the world" (190).

Another shock comes when Richard overhears his Uncle Tom warning his daughter—Richard's cousin Maggie—to stay away from him. Richard realizes that, in the past, he has wielded razors to keep his uncle's rage at bay, but he also knows that he is not a violent person, that he can be trusted. He deeply laments the way in which his family regards him. This feeling comes to include his own brother who, when he returns home from Chicago for a visit, seems, in Richard's eyes, to be held in higher regard by family members than he is. Estrangement between the brothers deepens, and not surprisingly, Richard's brother is afforded little presence in *Black Boy*.

46

Despite the array of hardships, Richard succeeds in school, and by the end of his junior high years, he is named valedictorian of his class and rewarded with an opportunity to make a speech at the graduation. The incident Wright describes, being denied the chance to read the speech he has prepared on his own and of being required instead to read the speech prepared by the principal, includes details whose veracity has been questioned by biographers. Specifically, biographer Michel Fabre asks the reader to consider a more complex situation than the one Wright relates in which his decision to stick with his own essay is a bold and noble act. Fabre's research uncovered a slightly different and more ethically delicate situation; namely, that the principal, Mr. Lanier, had, by strength of character and diplomacy, gained enough support from the white community to establish a high school for black students so their education would not cease with the completion of ninth grade. Mr. Lanier was concerned that Richard's speech might contain elements that would offend the supportive whites and that the plan of permanently establishing the school would ultimately fail. Suggestions that Wright might be denied his diploma if he did not cooperate, combined with his Uncle Tom's wrath and the enticement of a position teaching the school's lower grades, failed to break Richard's determination to read his own words. A compromise was reached when the principal reversed his decision, and Richard agreed to alter his text to eliminate elements that might antagonize the community. (For more information see *The Unfinished Quest of Richard Wright*, 1973.)

In Richard's account, he remains steadfast to the end, even borrowing money from his white employer to get a suit to wear to the graduation ceremony. Satisfied with his delivery of the speech, he once again leaves a community that has influenced him but that he nonetheless rejects, extending his feelings of alienation.

On his own and dependent on work to support himself, Wright has more occasion to both witness and experience everyday incidents of racism. Several of these are described in **chapter nine**. As a porter in a clothing store for black people,

Wright observes the ways the owners routinely abuse their customers, including overt expressions of disdain and physical assaults such as pushing and shoving. One incident stands out, however, that leaves Wright speechless: A woman who, as he later learns, is behind in her payments, is hauled into a back room by the owners and beaten until she begins to bleed. He is told this treatment is standard for black customers "when they don't pay their bills."

In a second incident, a group of white men traveling in a car appears to offer Wright a ride after his bicycle has broken down, but their intentions are anything but benign. When Wright has the audacity to refuse their offer of liquor, he is smashed in the head with a whiskey bottle and then flung from the car, entangled in his bike. Peering down at Wright on the ground they inform him that he has been lucky: If he had behaved toward another group of white men as he had with them, he would most likely be killed as a result. Later, a white policeman harasses him for making a delivery in a white neighborhood after dark, and his boss at the clothing store fires him for not laughing or talking like the other black patrons do. Wright explains that he does not laugh or talk because he finds nothing funny and has nothing to say.

Back on the streets, Wright encounters Griggs, a former classmate, who chastises him for acting improperly around whites. Calling it "[learning] how to live in the South," Griggs presents the tired and familiar argument that survival depends on convincing whites they are superior and upholding that impression and racial division at all times. Dick, as Griggs calls Richard, is viewed by others as too impatient and oblivious. While impatient, Wright is in actuality anything but oblivious. He has through the years achieved such a profound sense of himself—confident yet insecure at the same time—that he imagines that he does not notice "whiteness." Such a state presents a dilemma, Griggs believes. Wright is aware of the rigid and oppressive social codes regulating his behavior, but he longs to be free of this "plague" of excessive self-consciousness that forces him to act in a way contrary to his essential nature. He writes:

48

It was simply, utterly impossible for me to calculate, to scheme, to act, to plot all the time. I would remember to dissemble for short periods, then I would forget and act straight and human again, not with the desire to harm anybody, but merely forgetting the artificial status of race and class. It was the same with whites as with blacks; it was my way with everybody. (204)

Griggs ultimately reveals that he knows his argument is flawed, especially in the face of Wright's undeniably reckless, but more authentic posture. Griggs tries to illustrate his own "deep-down-in-my-heart" solidarity with Wright by reciting a crude little rhyme:

All these white folks dressed so fine
Their assholes smell just like mine. (204)

The issues raised by this dialogue between Griggs and Wright remaining unresolved, Griggs puts Wright in touch with a businessman from the North who is the proprietor of an optical shop and who wishes to train a black person in the trade. Wright gets the job, and his prospects begin to brighten until he tangles with two white employees—Pease and Reynolds—who harass Wright behind the boss's back for trying to "get smart" and "thinking [he's] white." The tensions escalate until they trap and taunt Wright over the false assertion that Wright had improperly addressed Pease. Forced into the position of being a liar or a provocateur and knowing either stance would elicit a beating with the metal bar Reynolds was holding, Wright leaves the shop. The friendly boss, Mr. Crane, is nowhere to be found. The next morning, Wright is summoned to Mr. Crane's office to report his view of the incident, but despite this official solicitude, Wright feels defeated. Outside the door of Mr. Crane's office, Reynolds lurks like an enraged beast ready to kill Wright the minute the boss is out of sight. Richard has bravely held despair at bay for a long time, but this time the odds are too great; he thinks of the recent fate of his friend's brother and succumbs for the first time to feelings of defeat. Mr. Crane assents reluctantly to Richard's decision to leave the job that had held real promise for him. "I'm going to get out of the South" is all Richard is able to say, and with more money from Mr. Crane than he has actually earned, Wright heads home. He has, at last, met a real ally, but one ally is not enough.

What must have been an experience akin to a nervous breakdown in Richard's life is described in **chapter ten**. The details—feelings of numbness and unreality, alienation from other human beings, chronic fatigue and lethargy, and reactivity—suggest a severe state of dissociation. Out of this extended fog comes an obsession to make enough money to get out of the South, but his desperation keeps him from making connections strong or long enough to be reliable sources of income. Wright creates in this chapter a convincing sense of what he felt in this state of mind that could be likened to a mental, psychological, and physical imprisonment. He moves along the streets like an animal expecting to be attacked, constantly switching between postures of assault and defense.

Richard explains this state of mind to himself as the result of having learning too late the "skill" of coping with the white world:

> I could not make subservience an automatic part of my behavior. I had to feel and think out each tiny item of racial experience in the light of the whole race problem, and to each problem I brought the whole of my life. While standing before a white man I had to figure out how to perform each act and how to say each word. . . . In the past I had always said too much, I found that it was difficult to say anything at all. (215)

Richard calls this state being "idle," but it resembles a form of paralysis. He has nonetheless arrived as a point of transition in his life and in the course of his autobiography.

An addition to Richard's beleaguered and bereft state is his observation of the way other blacks have become complicit in their own oppression. He notices—with a mix of contempt and envy—how easily his black peers slip into the roles whites prefer or indirectly demand they play. He comes across a young woman who thinks nothing of having a passing white man give her "a playful slap" on her buttocks, because she imagines herself having sufficient power to keep him from doing more.

Then he discovers how widespread thievery is among blacks against whites and how curiously easy it is to contemplate theft, despite the extra peril blacks risked in getting caught—certain conviction and the possibility of never even getting to the jail alive. Theft is, however, a grave move for Richard: "This was the first time in my life that I had ever seriously entertained the idea of violating the laws of the land. . . . I had not been dishonest from deliberate motives, but being dishonest had simply never occurred to me" (218). He now sees that fear on the part of blacks at the thought of organizing for higher wages has led to stealing as a kind of unstated compensation and protest. Worse, he comes to understand that many whites actually prefer blacks to steal rather than to pay them equal wages. This is an important insight for the times:

> But I, who wanted to look [whites] straight in the face, who wanted to talk and act like a man, inspired fear in them. The southern whites would rather have had Negroes who stole, work for them than Negroes who knew, however dimly, the worth of their own humanity. Hence, whites placed a premium upon black deceit; they encouraged irresponsibility; and their rewards were bestowed upon us blacks in the degree that we could make them feel safe and superior. (219)

Before joining the thieves, Richard performs intense self-analysis that brings him to the realization that his own learned inability to accommodate the white world on its own terms rendered white laws irrelevant to him: "I was outside those laws. The white people had told me so" (220). So with thoughts like—"I was gambling: freedom or the chain gang"—he responds to the cryptic remark—"We start tonight. . . . Are you with us?"—and joins the band of thieves. As a result, finally with enough money to leave, Richard seeks out his mother and tells her his plans. Briefly she resists, then relents, and sends him on his way.

Chapter eleven is an account of Richard's first week of real independence. Despite all the bravado, courage, and street smarts he has acquired through the years, he reveals an innocence both of youth and of prolonged rural life when he realizes that he is not always able to tell the difference between an actual boardinghouse and one that serves as a place of prostitution as well. By luck, it appears, a friendly and reassuring woman comes to his aid and offers him room and board for a sum he can afford. He makes an uncharacteristic show of territorial pride when she jokes about folks from Jackson not being known for their intelligence: "There are bright people in Jackson, too." More important is another discovery: "It was on reputably disreputable Beale Street in Memphis that I had met the warmest, friendliest person I had ever known, that I discovered that all human beings were not mean and driving, were not bigots like the rest of my family" (230).

Memphis brings additional surprises. Mrs. Moss and her daughter, Bess, are unrestrained and not shy in expressing their immediate trust in and affection for Richard, who is dumbfounded to find himself in the middle of a romantic plot. With a sense of relief, he gets a dishwashing job that frees him from their too-ardent plans. Richard almost lets himself be seduced by young Bess partly because he is overcome by the novelty of people expressing feelings so freely, quickly, and unabashedly. He thinks, "What kind of life had I lived that made the reality of this girl so strange?" In the end, he finds the situation so unexpected and strange that he makes an attempt to leave, which, taken as rejection by Bess, causes her to make a dramatic exit announcing to him, "I hate you!"

The next day, Richard has the kind of Beale Street experience he was partially expecting; unwittingly, he gets caught up in someone else's snare. "Last night I had found a naïve girl. This morning I had been a naïve boy," he observes (243). With remarks like this, one sees how Richard is unusual in being able to take note of his experiences in a way that enriches his self-awareness. He is a young man on a quest, and like other questing adventurers, Richard has an openness of mind and spirit that will unavoidably draw new people and experiences to him. He has already arrived at a point of maturity where he can imagine a goal in life that is not about money or power: making meaning out of meaningless suffering.

Although Memphis is a southern city, Richard finds in **chapter twelve** that its cultural makeup and diversity eases his tension about being around whites. In an optical shop at which he has wisely considered pursuing employment, he finds himself relatively comfortable among a variety of white urbanites—"Ku Klux Klanners to Jews . . . theosophists to just plain poor whites" (245). He wonders: "Either I could stand more mental strain than formerly or I had discovered deep within me ways of handling it" (245).

Back at the rooming house, Bess sulks and Mrs. Moss is sad and baffled by the wrong turn her plans have taken. Richard is even more baffled when within minutes Mrs. Moss goes from ordering him to move out for not having enough sense to marry her daughter to begging his forgiveness and promising no more of what had become for him an intolerable romantic melodrama.

Richard sets his mind to making enough money to be able to send some to his mother. In the tradition of the questing hero, Richard's vision, earnestness, and resolve are unwavering. He is also self-sacrificing—choosing to eat out of cans and to walk to work—so he has enough money for what matters most. After supporting his mother, finding books and magazine to read is his next priority, and he learns he can resell copies of *Harper's* and *The Atlantic Monthly* after he has finished them.

In the optical factory lunchroom, Richard observes his black co-workers engaging in conversations about every topic except their inability to initiate the actions that would allow them to get jobs of more equal standing to their white counterparts. Instead, they gossip and share petty complaints, also telling stories about little—and usually demeaning—ways they find to briefly outsmart their white colleagues. Richard listens to Shorty's story about getting a quarter out of a white man, but he is disgusted at the act of self-debasement it requires. Listening to this and other stories, Richard comes to recognize that the disproportionate amount of energy and thought many blacks used in order to secure the basic necessities of survival comes at the expense of the rest of their lives:

> If a white man had sought to keep us from obtaining a job, or enjoying the rights of citizenship, we would have bowed silently to his power. But if he had sought to deprive us of a dime, blood might have been spilt. Hence, our daily lives were so bound up with trivial objectives that to capitulate when challenged was tantamount to surrendering the right to life itself. . . . The lunch hour would pass and we would go back to work, but there would be in our faces not one whit of the sentiment we had felt during the hour of discussion. (251, 252)

The chapter ends with a bizarre episode that becomes emblematic of the existential condition of Richard Wright trying to grow up in the South. It begins when Mr. Olin, a foreman at the optical company, appears to befriend him by warning about a mortal threat coming from an employee of a rival optical business. The concept of "friend" associated with Mr. Olin, a man Richard barely knows and one who, moreover, has authority to take away his job, makes no sense, and Richard is immediately on guard. A consistent theme running through *Black Boy* has been the discovery that the outside world—for a black boy, especially a black boy with ambitions—almost always proves to be unworthy of trust.

The "rival," a young man named Harrison whom Richard knows even less than he knows Mr. Olin, is reported to have "a terrific grudge" against Richard. Richard is essentially paralyzed by this dilemma, because he knows that blacks can turn against one another to protect the job they have secured in a white-owned business. Richard is left to ponder: "Who was my friend: the white man or the black boy?" (257).

The threat intensifies, and the danger increases; Olin reports seeing Harrison outside waiting for Richard with a knife. Richard returns to work, but he is flooded with vexing questions and loses his appetite for lunch. Being black in the South carries the risk of having your life, with no warning and in a matter of seconds, threatened or taken from you. Richard thinks: "A white man had stepped into my delicately balanced world and had tipped it and I had to go right it before I could feel safe" (258). Reestablishing stability in his life turns out not to be possible despite a carefully and courageously choreographed attempt to do so. Richard approaches Harrison, who has been similarly warned, but neither young man can fully trust or reassure the other. Together, the pair figures out they have both been trapped by their white "superiors" into fearing the other in the hope of precipitating a fight among the two men—a common and despicable form of entertainment, frequently "arranged" or provoked by whites. In response, both men establish a separate and uneasy peace, vowing to not give in to being exploited in such a way. The harassment of the two keeps up for a week, and under this pressure, combined with the residual mistrust both carry and the enticement of five dollars each will receive as payment, they agree to relinquish their autonomy, sacrifice their integrity, and fight, assuring each other that it will be a "pretend" fight, a "cheating" fight that will trick the whites but will not end up harming or injuring either of them. The hope guiding this desperate but well-meaning pact is naïve; in the heat of the fight, each young man unleashes his own rage and mistrust, and both are injured. For four, brutal five-minute rounds, "the hate we felt for the men whom we had tried to cheat went into the blows we threw at each other" (265). This is the triumph of racism, and Richard knows it: "I felt that I had done something unclean, something for which I could never properly atone" (266).

In **chapter thirteen**, Richard discovers H.L. Mencken by chance. Wright is getting his customary "free read" in the bank lobby and notices a reference to Mencken in the Memphis *Commercial Appeal* in the form of an editorial castigating him. Richard is perplexed: "The only people I had ever heard denounced in the South were Negroes, and this man was not a Negro" (267). Despite the next scene embodying yet another denial and deprivation inflicted on southern blacks, it represents a small coup for Richard, another of the signs that his destiny to become a writer was irrevocably cast.

Denied access to the local library, Richard is denied the simple ability to read a book, specifically one written by H.L. Mencken. The two are a good match: Richard needs an ally in his own disavowal of racism, and Mencken was famously skilled at denouncing everything immoral, unjust, and hypocritical. Richard's scheme involves another act of duplicity; he must trick the librarian into getting Mencken's books out of the library and into his hands. He must calculate which of his fellow employees—one who is white and has a library card—is trustworthy. He chooses an Irish Catholic known to be a "pope lover" and thus not much liked by Protestant southerners. The man is at first reluctantly agreeable to the scheme (although he briefly appears to scare Richard into thinking his reading choices will be supervised) but then seems to enjoy aiding and abetting Richard's "transgression." Having run library errands for other whites before, Richard composes a note and forges a signature addressed to the librarian: "Dear Madam: Will you please let this nigger boy have some books by H. L. Mencken" (270). Richard knows he must use "nigger" to convince the librarian a white man is writing the note.

The scheme works, and Richard leaves with Mencken's *A Book of Prefaces and Prejudices.* That night, alone in his room, Richard begins to read, thereby entering a new realm—the world of books, learning, thinking, and criticizing, the world that will become his own. Struck by the novelty of clear and meaningful sentences, Richard makes his famous discovery of the power of words. "What was this?" he writes. The shock actually causes him to stand up, trying to grasp what new reality and meaning were contained in these words:

Yes, this man was fighting, fighting with words. He was using words as a weapon, using them as one would use a club. Could words be weapons? Well, yes, for here they were. Then, maybe, perhaps, I could use them as a weapon? No. It frightened me. I read on and what amazed me was not what he said, but how on earth anybody had the courage to say it. (272)

From this initial trigger comes a series of discoveries, each contained within the covers of the books he can now access. Through Mencken, Richard is introduced to Anatole France, Joseph Conrad, Sinclair Lewis, Sherwood Anderson, Feodor Dostoevsky, George Moore, Gustave Flaubert, Guy de Maupassant, Leo Tolstoy, Frank Harris, Mark Twain, Thomas Hardy, Arnold Bennett, Stephen Crane, Émile Zola, Frank Norris, Maxim Gorky, Henri-Louis Bergson, Henrik Ibsen, Honoré de Balzac, George Bernard Shaw, Alexander Dumas, Edgar Allan Poe, Thomas Mann, O. Henry, Theodore Dreiser, H.G. Wells, Nickolai Gogol, T.S. Eliot, André Gide, Charles Baudelaire, Edgar Lee Masters, Stendhal, Ivan Turgenev, James Huneker, Friedrich Nietzsche, and "scores of others." Though he cannot pronounce all their names and does not even know if these people are dead, alive, or ever existed, Richard has found his calling, his companions, and his new home. "[I had the feeling] of being affected by something that made the look of the world different" (273).

Most readers and critics praise Wright's autobiography for exposing and celebrating the power of literacy. One immediate effect for Richard comes by reading Sinclair Lewis's *Main Street*. Lewis's point of view alters Richard's reality; it empowers his sense of who he is in relationship to others. In this new light, his boss is transformed from a possessor of impersonal forces with formidable control over his life into a mere example of an "American type," burdened with "the very limits of his narrow life" (273).

This is an empowering insight. The transformation involves a reduction of the boss's personal power over Richard, who now has distance, a more objective view that frees him from one aspect of the bondage imposed by racism. "And all this happened because I had read a novel about a mythical man called George F. Babbitt" (273).

An inspired effort on Richard's part to start writing again fails, leaving him afraid that he will be denied the new life that has just opened before him:

> [how] was it possible to know people sufficiently to write about them? Could I ever learn about life and people? To me . . . my Jim Crow station in life [made it seem] a task impossible of achievement. I now knew what being a Negro meant. I could endure the hunger. I had learned to live with hate. But to feel that there were feelings denied me, that the very breath of life itself was beyond my reach, that more than anything else hurt. . . . I had a new hunger. (274)

As the chapter ends, it is clear to Richard that he is as alone as ever, that reading his books was just a way of "killing time." When, finally, he is joined by his mother and brother, who set up a comfortable home for themselves, Richard begins to eat better. With a return of the energy he had lost through his scrimping self-denying practices, he is able to envision himself continuing his quest. He calculates his chance for success if he stays in the South: minor triumphs through organizing with other blacks; becoming a "genial slave"; marriage to Bess and ownership of a house; forgetting and forgoing all that was offered in his discovery of literature and reading. None is acceptable. Still caught in his familiar anguish, Richard turns to thoughts of heading north.

In **chapter fourteen**, the final one of *Black Boy*, Richard embarks on the journey that has consumed his thoughts for so long. The decision is precipitated by the arrival of his Aunt Maggie who has been deserted by her shady boyfriend and is seeking a new life. Together, the four family members—Richard, his mother, brother, and Aunt Maggie—plot the move to Chicago and decide, sensibly: "if we waited until we were prepared to go, we would never leave" (278). The delicate process of informing his boss and co-workers of his intentions opens Richard up to a barrage of arguments, all intended to change his mind, all typically patronizing: It would be too cold; he might fall into "that lake"; he would not do any better "up there"; the "North's no good for [his people]"; and he's been "reading too many of them damn books" (280). Only two friends understand. His co-conspirator in the library gives him a "quick, secret smile," and Shorty, bitter about his own fate, says, "You lucky bastard" (281).

On the train north, Richard has time to reflect. Not surprisingly, he thinks of everything the South has done to hold him back, but, somewhat surprisingly, he concedes that, given the full force of that life-sapping oppression, he had "somehow" gotten the idea that life could be different. Still, a question lingers, and the answer is no clearer than it was at the beginning, despite how increasingly complex it has become: What, in essence, in the mixture of Jim Crow policies, family, the southern landscape, brushes with mortality, violence, terror, betrayal, and, above all, the hunger in all its manifestations that so deeply marked his life brought Wright to the place where the discovery of reading could be so liberating? Why, in brief, does Richard leave and Shorty knows he cannot?

Calling the South "the culture from which I sprang [and] the terror from which [he] fled," Richard has been sufficiently moved by the writers he has discovered to believe that change was possible, that "America could be shaped nearer to the hearts of those who lived in it" (283). If he can take the part of the South that is irrevocably within him and nurture it in different soil, then he might hold out the hope that "the South too could overcome its fear, its hate, its cowardice, its heritage of guilt and blood, its burden of anxiety and compulsive cruelty" (285).

All aspiring writers should get the last word. Richard heads north with these thoughts:

With ever watchful eyes and bearing scars, visible and invisible, I headed North, full of a hazy notion that life could be lived with dignity, that the personalities of others should not be violated, that men should be able to confront other men without fear or shame, and that if men were lucky in their living on earth they might win some redeeming meaning for their having struggled and suffered here beneath the stars (285).

Critical Views

W.E.B. DU BOIS ON WEAKNESSES IN *BLACK BOY*

This book tells a harsh and forbidding story and makes one wonder just exactly what its relation to truth is. The title, "A Record of Childhood and Youth," makes one at first think that the story is autobiographical. It probably is, at least in part. But mainly it is probably intended to be fiction or fictionalized biography. At any rate the reader must regard it as creative writing rather than simply a record of life.

The hero whom Wright draws, and maybe it is himself, is in his childhood a loathsome brat, foul-mouthed and "a drunkard." The family which he paints is a distressing aggregation. Even toward his mother he never expresses love or affection. Sometimes he comes almost to sympathy. He wonders why this poor woman, deserted by her husband, toiling and baffled, broken by paralysis and disappointment, should suffer as she does. But his wonder is intellectual inability to explain the suffering. It doesn't seem for a moment to be personal sorrow at this poor, bowed figure of pain and ignorance.

The father is painted as gross and bestial, with little of human sensibility. The grandmother is a religious fanatic, apparently sincere but brutal. The boy fights with his aunt. And here again the artist in Richard Wright seems to fail. He repeats an incident of fighting his aunt with a knife to keep her from beating him. He tells the tale of his grandfather, a disappointed veteran of the Civil War, but tells it without sympathy. The Negroes whom he paints have almost no redeeming qualities. Some work hard, some are sly, many are resentful; but there is none who is ambitious, successful or really intelligent.

After this sordid, shadowy picture we gradually come upon the solution. The hero is interested in himself, is self-centered to the exclusion of everybody and everything else. The suffering of others is put down simply as a measure of his own suffering and resentment. There is scarcely a ray of light in his childhood: he is hungry, he is beaten, he is cold and unsheltered. Above all, a naturally shy and introverted personality is forced back upon itself until he becomes almost pathological. The world is himself and his suffering. He hates and distrusts it. He says "I was rapidly learning to distrust everything and everybody."

He writes of a mother who wanted him to marry her daughter. "The main value in their lives was simple, clean, good living, and when they thought they had found those same qualities in one of their race they instinctively embraced him, liked him and asked no questions. But such simple unaffected trust flabbergasted me. It was impossible!"

He tells of his own pitiful confusion, when as an imaginative, eager child he could not speak his thought: "I knew how to write as well as any pupil in the classroom, and no doubt I could read better than any of them, and I could talk fluently and expressively when I was sure of myself. Then why did strange faces make me freeze? I sat with my ears and neck burning, hearing the pupils whisper about me, hating myself, hating them."

Then here and there for a moment he forgets his role as artist and becomes commentator and prophet. Born on a plantation, living in Elaine, Ark., and the slums of Memphis, he knows the whole Negro race! "After I had outlived the shocks of childhood, after the habit of reflection had been born in me, I used to mull over the strange absence of real kindness in Negroes, how unstable was our tenderness, how lacking in genuine passion we were, how void of great hope, how timid our joy, how bare our traditions, how hollow our memories, how lacking we were in those intangible sentiments that bind man to man, and how shallow was even our despair."

Not only is there this misjudgment of black folk and the difficult repulsive characters among them that he is thrown with, but the same thing takes place with white folk. There is not a single broad-minded, open-hearted white person in his book. One or two start out seemingly willing to be decent, but as he says of one white family for whom he worked, "They cursed each other in an amazingly offhand manner and nobody seemed to mind. As they hurled invectives they barely looked at each other. I was tense each moment, trying to anticipate their wishes and avoid a curse, and I did not suspect that the tension I had begun to feel that morning would lift itself into the passion of my life."

From the world of whites and the world of blacks he grows up curiously segregated. "I knew of no Negroes who read the books I liked, and I wondered if any Negroes ever thought of them. I knew that there were Negro doctors, lawyers, newspaper men, but I never saw any of them."

One rises from the reading of such a book with mixed thoughts. Richard Wright uses vigorous and straightforward English; often there is real beauty in his words even when they are mingled with sadism: "There was the disdain that filled me as I tortured a delicate, blue-pink crawfish that huddled fearfully in the mudsill of a rusty tin can. There was the aching glory in masses of clouds burning gold and purple from an invisible sun. There was the liquid alarm I saw in the blood-red glare of the sun's afterglow mirrored in the squared planes of whitewashed frame houses. There was the languor I felt when I heard green leaves rustling with a rainlike sound."

Yet at the result one is baffled. Evidently if this is an actual record, bad as the world is, such concentrated meanness, filth and despair never completely filled it or any particular part of it. But if the book is meant to be a creative picture and a warning, even then, it misses its possible effectiveness because it is as a work of art so patently and terribly overdrawn.

Nothing that Richard Wright says is in itself unbelievable or impossible; it is the total picture that is not convincing.

ISIDOR SCHNEIDER REVIEWS *BLACK BOY*

As autobiography *Black Boy* has all the faults of that riskiest form of writing; as a picture of the Negro people it is a distortion; but as a document of the psychological patterns of race tension it is unique, powerful and of considerable importance.

The fatal risk of autobiography is that the determination to tell the truth is frustrated by the accompanying impulse for self-preservation. The mind, fearful of its vulnerability in the nude, at once covers itself with justifications. That is why the heroes of autobiographies and of autobiographical fiction are generally nullities, cancelled out in the process of confession and simultaneous self-justification.

But Wright's form of self-justification also prevents him from realizing character in any other of his figures. They are all cast in active or passive phases of antagonism to him; all are obstacles to his self-fulfilment. By their antagonism he justifies his alienation. Their role is to serve the ego purpose of autobiography: "See what I have surmounted!"

What Mr. Wright reveals in *Black Boy* helps to explain his characteristics as a writer, his choice of material, his attitude toward people. The tension of conflict leaves its mark in the obsession with violence.

By the evidence in *Black Boy* these characteristics took form from some early childhood wound or maladjustment traceable only by a psychiatrist. We see them operating already in the child of four, as Wright recollects him, who sets fire to his house in retaliation for adult prohibitions. They are on view in the book in an almost unbroken record of hostility, cruelty, alienation, guilt sense, and violence.

The obsession with violence is particularly marked in Wright's early reading memories. This is how he recalls the story read to him by a friendly young woman boarder in his grandmother's house:

> She told how Bluebeard had duped and married his seven wives, how he had loved and slain them, how he had hanged them up by their hair in a dark closet. As she spoke reality changed, the look of things altered and the world became peopled with magical presences. My sense of life deepened and the feel of things was different somehow. Enchanted and enthralled, I stopped her constantly to ask for details. My imagination blazed. *The sensations the story aroused in me were never to leave me.* (My emphasis, I.S.)

In a similar vein he recalls a pulp serial in a newspaper that he sold it order to be able to read it:

> I was absorbed in the tale of a renowned scientist who had rigged up a mystery room made of metal in the basement of his palatial home. Prompted by some obscure motive he would lure his victims into this room and then throw an electric switch. Slowly, with heart-wracking agony, the air would be sucked from the metal room and his victims would die, turning red, blue, then black.

The chief significance in these passages lies not in Wright's enjoyment of such stories but in the place they have in his memory. They are the only early reading experiences recorded in detail and commented upon for their hold on his imagination. Indeed, as Wright notes, they never left his mind. In various forms the closet of crime, the torture chamber, the images of locked-in guilt, recur in Wright's fiction along with other fantasies of hostility and violence. What it fed on gives us the quality of Wright's imagination.

Hostility and alienation has not only kept Wright from intimate understanding and rounded presentation of individuals but also from sympathy with his people. There are derogatory epithets and allusions all through the book . . ."peasant," "wall-eyed yokels," "bleak pool of black life," etc. They are summed up in these parenthetical paragraphs printed early in the book:

> I used to mull over the strange absence of real kindness in Negroes, how unstable was our tenderness, how lacking in genuine passion we were, how void of great hope, how timid our joy, how bare our tradition, how hollow our memories, how lacking we were in those intangible sentiments that bind man to man, and how shallow was even our despair. After I had learned other ways of life I used to brood upon the unconscious irony of those who felt that Negroes led so passional an existence! I saw that what had been taken for our emotional strength was our negative confusions, our flights, our fears, our frenzy

under pressure. Whenever I thought of the essential bleakness of black life in America, I knew that Negroes had never been allowed to catch the full spirit of Western civilization, that they lived somehow in it but not of it. And when I brooded upon the cultural barrenness of black life, I wondered if clean positive tenderness, love, honor, loyalty, and the capacity to remember were native with man. I asked myself if these human qualities were not fostered, won, struggled and suffered for, preserved in ritual form from one generation to another.

Following out the implications of the last sentences one would have to assume doubts, on Wright's part, of Negro capacity for culture. Its existence could certainly not be proved from any testimony in the book. No reader would learn from it that there were any Negro cultural institutions or influences; or that Negro culture, even at the folk level, had made major contributions to American culture; or that a Douglass, a Carver, a Robeson had ever existed and stirred the Negro people; or that Negro struggle and protest was a proud strand in the American chronicle. It is, perhaps, no accident that Wright's own grandfather, who fought for Negro freedom as a Union soldier in the Civil War, is reduced to a ridiculous figure, bilked of his pension and presented, in possibly conscious symbolism, as somebody so impotent as not even to be of use to scare children into obedience.

Yet Wright's picture of bleak and shallow life is self-contradicted by episodes that the record compels him to set down. It would be difficult for any racial group to offer a finer example of deep feeling, of family solidarity and responsibility than his own far-scattered family who came in, some from Northern and Western towns, to assume the burdens brought by his mother's physical collapse. And it is contradicted in Wright's own book, written when he was a Communist, *Twelve Million Black Voices*.

Wright attempted to break out of the isolation that *Black Boy* defends by activities in the Communist Party. As published the book does not go into those years but it throws light on the chapters of recantation, published elsewhere, with which Wright brought that phase of his career to a squalid close. *Black Boy* renders any farther speculation on the causes unnecessary, as it renders his own self-justifications more specious and contradictory than was apparent at the time.

The causes which keep *Black Boy* from attaining stature as a work of art are the same which distort it as a picture of the Negro people. Yet its very concentration on the negative, the hostile, the violent, leads into explorations not attempted before. His innate interests heightened by a conscious interest in psycho-pathology, Wright makes keen observations of the neurotic behavior patterns and thought patterns produced by the race tensions in America. They form the major part of the second, and, by far, the most objective and successful part of the book. Set down with a sort of cold passion, they are powerfully and vividly realized. If is these contributions that give the book importance and a substantial compensating value.

LIONEL TRILLING ON THE TRAGIC SITUATION IN *BLACK BOY*

Richard Wright's "Black Boy" is a remarkably fine book. Perhaps a Negro's autobiography must always first appear under the aspect of sociology—a fact that is in itself a sociological comment—and "Black Boy" has its importance as a "document," a precise and no doubt largely typical account of Negro life in Mississippi. That it is the account of a tragic situation goes without saying. Here is the Negro poverty in all its sordidness; here is the calculated spiritual imprisonment of one racial group by another; here, above all, is the personal humiliation of Negro by white, the complex cruelty of the dominant race practiced as a kind of personal, spiritual necessity, sometimes direct and brutal, sometimes sophisticated with a sensual, guilty, horrible kindness.

But if "Black Boy" were no more than a document of misery and oppression, it would not have the distinction which in fact it does have. Our literature is full of autobiographical or reportorial or fictional accounts of misery and oppression. I am sure that these books serve a good purpose; yet I find that I feel a little coolness toward the emotions they generate, for it seems to me that too often they serve the liberal reader as a means of "escape." With honest kinds of "escape" there can be no quarrel—to find a moment's rest in dreams of heroic or erotic fulfilment is as justifiable as sleeping. But the moral "escape" that can be offered by accounts of suffering and injustice is quite another thing. To sit in one's armchair and be harrowed can all too easily pass far a moral or political action. We vicariously suffer in slippers and become virtuous: it is pleasant to exercise moral indignation at small cost; or to fill up emotional vacancy with good strong feeling at a safe distance; or to feel consciously superior to the brutal oppressor; or to be morally entertained by poverty, seeing it as a new and painful kind of primitivism which tenderly fosters virtue, or, if not virtue, then at least "reality"; or to indulge in self-pity by projecting it—very pleasant, very flattering, a little corrupting. Mr. Wright's autobiography, so far as it is an account of misery and oppression, does not tempt its readers to such pleasures. This is the mark of the dignity and integrity of the book.

In other words, the sociological aspect of "Black Boy" is the field—I will not say *merely* the field—for a notable exercise of the author's moral and intellectual power. It is difficult to describe that power except, as I have tried to do, by speaking of its effect, by remarking that it does not lead us into easy and inexpensive emotions, although the emotions into which it does lead us are durable. If I try further to understand this, I can only surmise that it comes about because the author does not wholly identify himself with his painful experience, does not, therefore, make himself a mere object of the reader's consciousness, does not make himself that different kind of human being, a "sufferer." He is not an object, he is a subject; he is the same kind of person as his reader, as complex, as free.

"Black Boy" is an angry book, as it ought to be. I would be surprised and unhappy if it were not. But the amount of anger that Mr. Wright feels is in proportion only to the social situation he is dealing with; it is also in proportion to the author's desire to live a reasonable and effective life. For what a Negro suffers in the South—what, indeed, he might suffer in the North—calls for illimitable anger. But the full amount of anger that would be appropriate to the social situation alone would surely have the effect of quite destroying the person who felt it. And Mr. Wright, almost from infancy, seems to have refused to be destroyed. For example, by what, as he describes it, seems to have been a kind of blessed unawareness, even a benign stupidity, he simply could not understand the difference between black people and white. That his grandmother was so white as to be almost white may have had something to do with it. In any case, the young Richard had to be taught the difference, and it seems to have been at best a learned thing. This, to be sure, could scarcely have protected him from all psychic wounds and scars. But although he suffered, he seems never to have been passive. He seems thus to have been saved from the terrible ambivalences of the oppressed, from the self-indulgence, the self-pity, the ripe luxuriousness of sensitivity; and he does not, as the oppressed so often do, give himself or his oppressors a false glamour.

Mr. Wright's autobiography does not go beyond the time when he left the South at the age of nineteen. To me this is a disappointment, for Mr. Wright's life after his departure from the South is a great theme—the entrance of an aspiring and relatively ignorant young man into the full stream of national life is always a subject of the richest social and moral interest, and Mr. Wright's race makes that interest the richer. The chapters which appeared in the *Atlantic Monthly* under the title "I Tried to Be a Communist" are not included in "Black Boy"; they are not so interesting as they might be, although they have their point, but they suggest the kind of cultural and social experience I should like to see Mr. Wright explore. He has the directness and honesty to do it well. He has the objectivity which comes from refusing to be an object.

It is this objectivity that allows Mr. Wright to believe that oppression has done something more than merely segregate his people. He dares, that is, to take the oppression seriously, to believe that it really does oppress, that its tendency is not as much to exempt the oppressed from the moral flaws of the dominant culture from which they are excluded as it is to give them other flaws of feeling and action. He himself suffered from the fierce puritanical religiosity of his own family. He can speak tenderly of the love that his mother gave him, but he can speak with sorrow and bitterness of the emotional bleakness in which he was reared. . . .

I suppose that it is for saying this, of other things of a similar objectivity that Mr. Wright has, as I have heard come under the fire of his own people. And that, perhaps, is understandable But if, like Mr. Wright, we believe that oppression is real, we must sadly praise his courage in seeing that it does not merely affect the body but also the soul. It is only a grim and ironic justice that the deterioration is as great in the oppressor as in the oppressed.

RALPH ELLISON ON THE ORIGINS OF RICHARD WRIGHT'S SENSIBILITY

If anybody ask you
  who sing this song,
Say it was ole [Black] Boy
  done been here and gone.[1]

As a writer, Richard Wright has outlined for himself a dual role: To discover and depict the meaning of Negro experience and to reveal to both Negroes and whites those problems of a psychological and emotional nature which arise between them when they strive for mutual understanding.

Now, in *Black Boy*, he has used his own life to probe what qualities of will, imagination, and intellect are required of a southern Negro in order to possess the meaning of his life in the United States. Wright is an important writer, perhaps the most articulate Negro American, and what he has to say is highly perceptive. Imagine Bigger Thomas projecting his own life in lucid prose, guided, say, by the insights of Marx and Freud, and you have an idea of this autobiography.

Published at a time when any sharply critical approach to Negro life has been dropped as a wartime expendable, it should do much to redefine the problem of the Negro and American democracy. Its power can be observed in the shrill manner with which some professional "friends of the Negro people" have attempted to strangle the work in a noose of newsprint.

What in the tradition of literary autobiography is it like, this work described as a "great American autobiography"? As a nonwhite intellectual's statement of his relationship to Western culture, *Black Boy* recalls the conflicting pattern of identification and rejection found in Nehru's *Toward Freedom*. In its use of fictional techniques, its concern with criminality (sin) and the artistic sensibility, and in its author's judgment and rejection of the narrow world of his origin, it recalls Joyce's rejection of Dublin in *A Portrait of the Artist*. And as a psychological document of life under oppressive conditions, it recalls *The House of the Dead*, Dostoyevsky's profound study of the humanity of Russian criminals.

Such works were perhaps Wright's literary guides, aiding him to endow his life's incidents with communicable significance, providing him with ways of seeing, feeling, and describing his environment. These influences, however, were encountered only after these first years of Wright's life were past and were not part of the immediate folk culture into which he was born. In that culture the specific folk-art form that helped shape the writer's attitude toward his life and that embodied the impulse that contributes much to the quality and tone of his autobiography was the Negro blues. This would bear a word of explanation:

The blues is an impulse to keep the painful details and episodes of a brutal experience alive in one's aching consciousness, to finger its jagged grain, and to transcend it, not by the consolation of philosophy, but by squeezing from it a near-tragic, near-comic lyricism. As a form, the blues is an autobiographical chronicle of personal catastrophe expressed lyrically. And certainly Wright's early childhood was crammed with catastrophic incidents. In a few short years his father deserted his mother, he knew intense hunger, he became a drunkard begging drinks from black stevedores in Memphis saloons; he had to flee Arkansas where an uncle was lynched; he was forced to live with a fanatically religious grandmother in an atmosphere of constant bickering; he was lodged in an orphan asylum; he observed the suffering of his mother who became a permanent invalid, while fighting off the blows of the poverty-stricken relatives with whom he had to live; he was cheated, beaten, and kicked off jobs by white employees who disliked his eagerness to learn a trade; and to these objective circumstances must be added the subjective fact that Wright, with his sensitivity, extreme shyness, and intelligence was a problem child who rejected his family and was by them rejected.

Thus along with the themes, equivalent descriptions of milieu, and the perspectives to be found in Joyce, Nehru, Dostoyevsky, George Moore, and Rousseau, *Black Boy* is filled with blues-tempered echoes of railroad trains, the names of southern towns and cities, estrangements, fights and flights, deaths and disappointments, charged with physical and spiritual hungers and pain. And like a blues sung by such an artist as Bessie Smith, its lyrical prose evokes the paradoxical, almost surreal image of a black boy singing lustily as he probes his own grievous wound.

In *Black Boy*, two worlds have fused, two cultures merged, two impulses of western man become coalesced. By discussing some of its cultural sources I hope to answer those critics who would make of the book a miracle and of its author a mystery. And while making no attempt to probe the mystery of the artist (who Hemingway says is "forged in injustice as a sword is forged") I do hold that basically the prerequisites to the writing of *Black Boy* were, on the one hand, the microscopic degree of cultural freedom that Wright found in the South's stony injustice and, on the other, the existence of a personality agitated to a state of almost manic restlessness. There were, of course, other factors, chiefly ideological; but these came later.

Wright speaks of his journey north as

. . . taking a part of the South to transplant in alien soil, to see if it could grow differently, if it could drink of new and cool rains, bend in strange winds, respond to the warmth of other suns, and perhaps, to bloom. . . .

And just as Wright, the man, represents the blooming of the delinquent child of the autobiography, just so does *Black Boy* represent the flowering—cross-fertilized by pollen blown by the winds of strange cultures—of the humble blues lyric. There is, as in all acts of creation, a world of mystery in this, but there is also enough that is comprehensible for Americans to create the social atmosphere in which other black boys might freely bloom.

For certainly, in the historical sense, Wright is no exception. Born on a Mississippi plantation, he was subjected to all those blasting pressures which, in a scant eighty years, have sent the Negro people hurtling, without clearly defined trajectory, from slavery to emancipation, from log cabin to city tenement, from the white folks' fields and kitchens to factory assembly lines; and which, between two wars, have shattered the wholeness of its folk consciousness into a thousand writhing pieces.

Black Boy describes this process in the personal terms of one Negro childhood. Nevertheless, several critics have complained that it does not "explain" Richard Wright. Which, aside from the notion of art involved, serves to remind us that the prevailing mood of American criticism has so thoroughly excluded the Negro that it fails to recognize some of the most basic tenets of western democratic thought when encountering them in a black skin. They forget that human life possesses an innate dignity and mankind an innate sense of nobility; that all men possess the tendency to dream and the compulsion to make their dreams reality; that the need to be ever dissatisfied and the urge ever to seek satisfaction is implicit in the human organism; and that all men are the victims and the beneficiaries of the goading, tormenting, commanding, and informing activity of that process known as the Mind—the Mind, as Valéry describes it, "armed with its inexhaustible questions."

Perhaps all this (in which lies the very essence of the human, and which Wright takes for granted) has been forgotten because the critics recognize neither Negro humanity nor the full extent to which the southern community renders the fulfillment of human destiny impossible. And while it is true that *Black Boy* presents an almost unrelieved picture of a personality corrupted by brutal environment, it also presents those fresh human responses brought to its world by the sensitive child:

> There was the *wonder* I felt when I first saw a brace of mountainlike, spotted, black-and-white horses clopping down a dusty road . . . the *delight* I caught in seeing long straight rows of red and green vegetables stretching away in the sun . . . the faint, cool kiss of *sensuality* when dew came on to my cheeks . . . the vague sense of *the infinite* as I looked down upon the yellow, dreaming waters of the Mississippi . . . the echoes of *nostalgia* I heard in the crying strings of wild geese . . . the *love* I had for the mute regality of tall, moss-clad oaks . . . the hint of *cosmic cruelty* that I felt when I saw the curved timbers of a wooden shack that had been warped in the summer sun . . . and there was the *quiet terror* that suffused my senses when vast hazes of gold washed earthward from star-heavy skies on silent nights . . . [2]

And a bit later, his reactions to religion:

> Many of the religious symbols appealed to my sensibilities and I responded to the dramatic vision of life held by the church, feeling that to live day by day with death as one's sole thought was to be so compassionately sensitive toward all life as to view all men as slowly dying, and the trembling sense of fate that welled up, sweet and melancholy, from the hymns blended with the sense of fate that I had already caught from life.

There was also the influence of his mother—so closely linked to his hysteria and sense of suffering—who (though he only implies it here) taught him, in the words of the dedication prefacing *Native Son*, "to revere the fanciful and the imaginative." There were also those white men—the one who allowed Wright to use his library privileges and the other who advised him to leave the South, and still others whose offers of friendship he was too frightened to accept.

Wright assumed that the nucleus of plastic sensibility is a human heritage—the right and the opportunity to dilate, deepen, and enrich sensibility—democracy. Thus the drama of *Black Boy* lies in its depiction of what occurs when Negro sensibility attempts to fulfill itself in the undemocratic South. Here it is not the individual that is the immediate focus, as in Joyce's Stephen Hero, but that upon which his sensibility was nourished.

Notes
1. Signature formula used by blues singers at conclusion of song.
2. Italics mine.

George E. Kent Offers Some Thoughts on Richard Wright's Autobiography

The main source for information concerning Wright's early youth is still *Black Boy*, a great autobiography, but one whose claim to attention is the truth of the artist, and not that of the factual reporter. Both Ralph Ellison and Constance Webb, Wright's biographer, have identified incidents which Wright did not personally experience, incidents from folk tradition.[3] I see no great to-do to be made over Wright's artistic license, since folk tradition is the means by which a group expresses its deepest truths. Thus the picture, if not all the pieces, is essentially true.

What *Black Boy* reveals is that more than any other major black writer, Wright, in his youth, was close to the black masses—and in the racially most repressive state in the union, Mississippi. Worse still, Wright received violent suppression without the easement provided by the moral bewilderment and escapism so available in black culture. Such institutionalized instruments of bewilderment as the otherworldly religion, the smiling side of the "good" white folks, sex, liquor, and the warmth of the folk culture, formed no sustaining portion of his psychic resources. Parents, whose complicity in oppression made for physical security in the South of the pre–and post–World War I periods, were ineffectual. Wright's father was a zero. His mother—a woman bearing up under tensions from the terrors of the daily world, abandonment by a shiftless husband, and painful and disabling sickness—was hard-pressed by Wright and her own tough-minded honesty. Under a persistent barrage of questions concerning black life, answers escaped her lips that merely confirmed the boy's sense of embattlement in a world of naked terror; first, for example, explaining that a white man did not whip a black boy because the black boy was his son, she then sharpened a distinction: "The 'white' man did not *whip* the 'black' boy. He *beat* the 'black' boy.'[4]

Constance Webb states Wright's conscious purpose: "to use himself as a symbol of all the brutality and cruelty wreaked upon the black man by the Southern environment."[5] By depressing his middle-class background, Miss Webb continues, he would create a childhood that would be representative of most Negroes. Both the power of the autobiography and its flaws develop from Wright's single-minded intention. Actually, for much of the work, his strategy is to posit a self-beyond-culture—that is, the self as biological fact, a very tough biological fact, indeed. A cosmic self, which reaches out naturally (though in twisted and violent patterns) for the beauty and nobleness of life. The self is battered by the white racist culture, and, for the most part, by a survival-oriented black culture, that counters the impulse to rebelliousness and individuality by puritanical repressiveness, escapism, and base submission. That is, black culture suppressed the individual, in order to protect the group from white assault. The dramatic rendering of these forces and the stubborn persistence of the outsider self comprise the major strategy of the book.

And out of that strategy comes an overwhelming impact. Tension, raw violence and impending violence, which evoke, psychologically, a nightmare world in the light of day. The autobiography's first great subject is the growth of consciousness, the stages of which are communicated by statements of the reactions of self to preceding events. In confronting a racist America the black boy's consciousness learns to hide its responses and to pursue its aspirations by secret means. It is damaged for life, but it has avoided becoming a natural product of the system: the stunted, degraded, shuffling black, almost convinced of its own inferiority and the god-like power of whites. In the latter part of the book, through reading rebellious books, the consciousness of that other self—the white-defined Negro-victim—loses ground to the consciousness of self as American: the heir to the energy releasing resources of the Enlightenment. A desperate hope is created.

Thus *Black Boy*'s second great subject: the disinherited attempting to reclaim the heritage of Modern Man.

Black Boy is a great social document, but it could easily have been greater. Its simple naturalistic form, at first, knocks the reader off balance, but then comes reflection. Its universe of terror is little relieved by those moments of joy that usually glide like silent ancestral spirits into the grimmest childhood. To account artistically for the simple survival of the narrator is difficult. Except for the "cultural transfusion" that the narrator receives near the end, Wright gives little artistic emphasis to cultural supports. The careful reader will pick up, here and there, scattered clues. For example, the extended family, with all its short-comings, show a desperate energy and loyalty. Reading was an early feeder of his imaginative life, and the role of his mother in supplying imaginative and emotional help was crucial. In *Black Boy*, the dramatic form does not, in itself, give her a decisive role, but the beatings, teasings, grim love and sporadic periods of silent understanding, imply an unorthodox devotion. The narrator reveals something of the sort in stating the impact of her sickness upon him:

Already there had crept into her speech a halting, lisping quality that, though I did not know it, was the shadow of her future. I was more conscious of my mother now than I had ever been and I was already able to feel what being completely without her would mean.[6]

There were important facets of ordinary black life, which Wright did not understand because he saw them as an outsider or from the point of view of embattled adolescence. His father was simply the peasant-victim, with a life shaped by the rhythms of the seasons—a classification very likely to have been derived from his Marxian studies. In Memphis, Wright (or the narrator) meets Mrs. Moss, a spontaneously warm and generous black woman, with an equally warm and spontaneous daughter, Bess. Bess likes Richard and, in no time flat, wishes to marry him. The narrator is aware of her qualities, but ascribes their source to what he was later to understand as "the peasant mentality."

Yet this warm spontaneity, as much as the warped puritanism of his own environment, was a value bulwarked and preserved by the embattled black cultural tradition—not by nature or the rhythm of the seasons. Thus the utter bleakness of black life, its lack of tenderness, love, honor, genuine passion, etc., which Wright in a now famous passage in the second chapter of the autobiography noted as general characteristics, were partly reflections of his immediate home life and surroundings: "I had come from a home where feelings were never expressed, except in rage or religious dread, where each member of the household lived locked in his own dark world, and the light that shone out of this child's heart [Bess's] . . . blinded me."[7]

Personal tension and the double-consciousness. In response to white definitions, Wright was able to say to whites that he formed an equation not known in their definitions. Regarding his people, he was able to say that they are much like you define them but you, and not Nature, are responsible. If today, this no longer seems enough to say, or even to be free of a certain adolescent narcissism, we can at least concentrate upon what insights should have been available to Wright during his time. If Wright in *Black Boy* seems too much concerned with warfare upon white definitions, it is good to remember that our growing ability to ignore them exists because the single-minded assault of Wright and others shook up the confidence of a nation and impaired their efficiency.

What can be held against him is that he seemed to have had little awareness that black life, on its own terms, has also the measure of beauty and grandeur granted those who are often defeated but not destroyed.

Notes

3. See Ralph Ellison, *Shadow and Act* (New York, 1964), pp. 134–135; Constance Webb, *Richard Wright* (New York, 1968), p. 205. See also notes to this Chapter (XIV). From Miss Webb's discussion of *Black Boy*, I deduce that he was still too close psychologically to his youth to give a rounded picture. [Michel Fabre's 1973 biography has filled some of the lacunae in the history of Wright's early development. *Eds.*]

4. Richard Wright, *Black Boy* (New York, 1945), p. 52.

5. Webb, p. 205.

6. *Black Boy*, p. 73.

7. *Ibid.*, p. 190.

HORACE A. PORTER ON RICHARD WRIGHT AND THE POWER OF WORDS

Although critics have discussed the effect of Wright's early life on his writings, none has shown systematically how *Black Boy* (and to a lesser degree *American Hunger*) can be read primarily as a portrait of the artist as a young man. Consequently, I intend to demonstrate how the theme of words (with their transforming and redeeming power) is the nucleus around which ancillary themes swirl. Wright's incredible struggle to master words is inextricably bound to his defiant quest for individual existence and expression. . . . What one sees in Wright's autobiographies is how the behavior of his fanatically religious grandmother, the painful legacy of his father, the chronic suffering of his mother, and how his interactions with blacks and whites both in and outside his immediate community are all thematically connected to the way Wright uses words to succeed as a writer and as a man. . . .

What has been characterized as ritual parricide comes readily to mind when Wright's father is awakened one day by the meowing of a stray cat his sons have found. Wright's father screams at him and his brother: "'Kill that damn thing!'" His father shouts, "'Do anything, but get it away from here!'" Ignoring the advice of his brother, Wright does exactly what his father suggests. He puts a rope around the cat's neck and hangs it. Why? Wright explains:

> I had had my first triumph over my father. I had made him believe that I had taken his words literally. He could not punish me now without risking his authority. I was happy because I had at last found a way to throw criticism of him into his face. I had made him feel that, if he whipped me for killing the kitten, I would never give serious weight to his words again. I had made him know that I felt he was cruel and I had done it without his punishing me.[6]

Young Wright's cunning act of interpretation is the telling point here. If one were dubious about the meaning of the son's act of arson, the passage cited above demonstrates a full-blown hatred and contempt. But note how Wright focuses on his father's words, how he attempts to neutralize his father's psychological authority by a willful misinterpretation of his statement. . . .

Wright's mother also plays an important role in this psychological scheme of reconciliation and vindication. Despite the fact that his mother whipped him until he was unconscious after he set the house afire, he expresses tenderness toward her throughout *Black Boy*; Wright informs the reader that his mother was the first person who taught him to read and told him stories. After Wright had hanged the kitten in order to triumph over his father, he explains that his mother, who is "more imaginative, retaliated with an assault upon my sensibilities that crushed me with the moral horror involved in taking a life."[9] His mother makes him bury the kitten that night and makes him pray. . . .

Words lead to Wright's salvation and to his redemption. From the first pages of *Black Boy*, the reader witnesses Wright at the tender, impressionable age of six becoming a messenger of the obscene. One day a black man drags Wright, who is peering curiously through the doors of a saloon, inside. The unscrupulous and ignorant adults give him liquor and send obscene messages by him back and forth to one another. Wright goes from one persons to the next shouting various obscenities in tune to the savage glee and laughter of the crowd. Surely, the incident makes Wright, inquisitive as he is, wonder about the odd effects of his words.

He later learns his first lesson on the power of the written word. Returning home after his first day of school during which he had learned "all the four-letter words describing physiological and sex functions," from a group of older boys, he decides to display his newly acquired knowledge. Wright goes from window to window in his neighborhood and writes the words in huge soap letters. A woman stops him and drives him home. That night the same woman informs his mother of what Wright calls his "inspirational scribblings." As punishment, she takes him out into the night with a pail of water and a towel and demands that he erase the words he had written: "'Now scrub until that word's gone,' she ordered."

This comical incident may appear insignificant on the surface. Furthermore, one cannot know the nature or the degree of the psychological effect the incident had on Wright. However, it seems reasonable to assume that it had a significant psychological impact. As Wright presents it, it is the first occasion on which words he writes are publicly censored; the first incident during which family members and neighbors become angry, if amused, because of words he writes. Wright states: "Neighbors gathered, giggling, muttering words of pity and astonishment, asking my mother how on earth I could have learned so much so quickly. I scrubbed at the four-letter soap words and grew blind with anger."[13]

Wright's first written words are not the only words to get him in trouble. His first exposure to imaginative literature also causes a scene. One day a young school teacher, who boards with his grandmother, read to him *Bluebeard and His Seven Wives*. Wright describes the effect that the story has on him in visionary terms: "The tale made the world around me, throb, live. As she spoke reality changed, the look of things altered, and the world became peopled with magical presences. My sense of life deepened and the feel of things was different, somehow. Enchanted and enthralled. . . ."[14]

Wright's visionary, enchanted state does not last. His grandmother screams "'you stop that you evil gal!' . . . 'I want none of that devil stuff in my house!'" When Wright insists that he likes the story and wants to hear what happened, his grandmother tells him, "'you're going to burn in hell. . . . '" Wright reacts strongly to this incident. He promises himself that when he is old enough, he "would buy all the novels there were and read them." Not knowing the end of the tale fills Wright with "a sense of emptiness and loss." He states that the tale struck "a profoundly responsive chord" in him:

> So profoundly responsive a chord had the tale struck in me that the threats of my mother and grandmother had no effect whatsoever. They read my insistence as mere obstinacy, as foolishness, something that would quickly pass; and they had no notion how desperately serious the tale had made me. They could not have known that Ella's whispered story of deception and murder had been the first experience in my life that had elicited from me a total emotional response. No words or punishment could have possibly made me doubt. I had tasted what to me was life, and I would have more of it somehow, some way. . . . [15]

. . . Against the wishes of the community, Wright continues to read and develop as a young writer. His first real triumph comes when the editor of the local Negro newspaper accepts one of Wright's stories, "The Voodoo of Hell's Half-Acre." The plot of the story involves a villain who wants a widow's home. After the story is published, no one, excepting the newspaper editor, gives any encouragement. His grandmother calls it "'the devil's work'"; his high school principal objects to his use of "hell" in the story's title; even his mother feels that his writing will make people feel that he is "weak minded." His classmates do not believe that he has written the story:

> They were convinced that I had not told them the truth. We had never had any instruction in literary matters at school; the literature of the nation of the Negro had never been mentioned. My schoolmates could not understand why I had called it *The Voodoo of Hell's Half-Acre*. The mood out of which a story was written was the most alien thing conceivable to them. They looked at me with new eyes, and a distance, a suspiciousness came between us. If I had thought anything in writing the story, I had thought that perhaps it would make me more acceptable to them, and now it was cutting me off from them more completely than ever.[19]

Herein, Wright identifies another problem which menaces him throughout his writing life. The problem is the young artist's radical disassociation of sensibility from that of the group. In this regard, he is reminiscent of the young artist heroes of Mann and Joyce, of Tonio Kröger and Stephen Daedalus. However, Wright's plight as a young artist is significantly different in a crucial way. His is not simply the inability to experience, by dint of his, poetic sensibility, "the blisses of the commonplace." Not only is Wright pitted against his immediate family and community, the tribe, as he calls them. He must also fight against the prejudices of the larger society.

Wright wrote "The Voodoo of Hell's Half-Acre" when he was fifteen. He concludes:

> Had I been conscious of the full extent to which I was pushing against the current of my environment, I would have been frightened altogether out of my attempts at writing. . . .
>
> I was building up in me a dream which the entire educational system of the South had been rigged to stifle. I was feeling the very thing that the state of Mississippi

had spent millions of dollars to make sure that I would never feel; I was becoming aware of the thing that the Jim Crow laws had been drafted and passed to keep out of my consciousness; I was acting on impulses that Southern senators in the nation's capital had striven to keep out of Negro life. . . . [20]

A telling example which brilliantly demonstrates what Wright means in the passage cited above involves his love for words and books once again. When Wright is nineteen, he reads an editorial in the Memphis *Commercial Appeal* which calls H. L. Mencken a fool. Wright knows that Mencken is the editor of the *American Mercury* and he wonders what Mencken has done to deserve such scorn. How can he find out about Mencken? Since blacks are denied the right to use the public libraries, he is not permitted to check out books. But Wright proves both ingenious and cunning.

He looks around among his co-workers at the optical company where he is employed and chooses the white person— a Mr. Falk—who he thinks might be sympathetic. The man is an Irish Catholic, "a pope lover" as the white Southerners say. Wright had gotten books from the library for him several times, and wisely figures that since he too is hated, he might be somewhat sympathetic. Wright's imagination and courage pays off. Although somewhat skeptical about Wright's curious request from the outset, Mr. Falk eventually gives Wright his card, warning him of the risk involved and swearing him to secrecy. Wright promises that he will write the kind of notes Mr. Falk usually writes and that he will sign Falk's name.

Since Wright does not know the title of any of Mencken's books, he carefully composes what he considers a foolproof note: "*Dear Madam: Will you please let this nigger have some books by H. L. Mencken.*"[21] The librarian returns with Mencken's *A Book of Prefaces and Prejudices*. His reading of Mencken provides him with a formidable reading list: Anatole France, Joseph Conrad, Sinclair Lewis, Sherwood Anderson, Dostoevski, George Moore, Flaubert, Maupassant, Tolstoy,

Frank Harris, Twain, Hardy, Crane, Zola, Norris, Gorky, Bergson, Ibsen, Shaw, Dumas, Poe, Mann, Dreiser, Eliot, Gide, Stendhal, and others. Wright starts reading many of the writers Mencken mentions. Moreover, the general effect of his reading was to make him more obsessive about it: "Reading grew into a passion. . . . Reading was like a drug, a dope."[22]

Mencken provides Wright with far more than a convenient reading list of some of the greater masters. He becomes an example to Wright—perhaps an idol—both in matters of style and vocational perspective or stance:

> I opened *A Book of Prefaces* and began to read. I was jarred and shocked by the style, the clear, clean, sweeping sentences. Why did he write like that? And how did one write like that? I pictured the man as a raging demon, slashing with his pen, consumed with hate, denouncing everything American, extolling everything European or German, laughing at the weaknesses of people, mocking God, authority. What was this? I stood up, trying to realize what reality lay behind the meaning of the words. . . . Yes, this man was fighting, fighting with words. He was using words as a weapon, using them as one would use a club. Could words be weapons? Well, yes, for here they were. Then, maybe, perhaps, I could use them as a weapon.[23]

Notes

6. *Ibid.*, 10–11.
9. *Ibid.*, 11.
13. *Ibid.*, 22.
14. *Ibid.*, 34.
15. *Ibid.*, 36.
19. *Ibid.*, 146.
20. *Ibid.*, 148.
21. *Ibid.*, 216.
22. *Ibid.*, 218–19.
23. *Ibid.*, 218.

> Personal evolution is always a struggle between the
> Individual and society—a struggle for self-expression on
> the part of the individual, for his subjection, on the part
> of society—and it is in the total course of this struggle
> that the personality—not as a static 'essence' but as a
> dynamic, continuing evolving set of activity—manifests
> and constructs itself.

With these words Thomas and Znaniecki, two early Chicago
sociologists, postulated a dichotomy which is crucial to the
understanding of *Black Boy* and *American Hunger*.[12] This
notion constitutes the common ground on which a sociological
theory and a literary text stand: the former articulating and
evolving it into a set of concepts and categories, the latter
dramatizing it and demonstrating its functioning in the
concrete details of a life-story.

The struggle between individual and society forms the
backbone of Wright's autobiography, just as it controls the two
main categories used in the text—the concept of "personality"
and the concept of "environment." "Environment" here becomes
an all inclusive term, indicating the group, the community, the
culture, tradition, authority. Against these formidable institutions
and the threats which they produce, the individual "personality"
must strive for self-realization. These institutions become
tangible living bodies, more real than the single individuals who
form them. They are the formidable challenges against which
Richard Wright, the only individual who seems consciously to
oppose the racist South, must contend.

In *Black Boy* and *American Hunger* three types of institutions
confront the individual and organize his life-story: the family to
which he belongs by blood; the South—epitomized by religion,
school, and the racist white world—to which he belongs by
culture; and the Communist Party to which he belongs by
choice. As a ritual reenactment of the pyromaniacal action of

the first scene, the autobiography develops through numberless episodes in which the hero sets symbolic fires to the institutions which surround him. This seems to be the only way to keep his personality intact, until the choice of isolation, which closes the autobiography, emerges as the only alternative to the oppression of the group.

The hero's relationship with the family covers the first half of *Black Boy*. It develops through a progression from passive to resentful submission, to successful rebellion against the authority of this institution and of the entire family environment. Attempts at self-expression provide the ground for most of the confrontations. Young Richard is punished for printing "four-letter words describing physiological and sex-functions" which he had just learned in school (pp. 32–33). He is punished for listening to the "Devil's stuff," the story of Bluebeard and His Seven Wives (p. 47). He is punished for speaking words "whose meaning he did not fully know. 'When you get through, kiss back there,' he said, the words rolling softly but unpremeditatedly" (p. 49). Many other times he is "slapped across the mouth" for saying something wrong.

Far from being a simple catalogue of beatings and punishments, the narrative illustrates the child's growing ability to rebel against his environment and its institutions, and describes the process through which his personality shapes itself and is in turn shaped. Moreover, each time he successfully emerges from a confrontation with a family member, the hero is able to keep his personality intact only through a progressive denial of kinship and through a growing sense of isolation. In the first confrontation with his father, the narrator describes the old man as a "stranger to me, always somehow alien and remote" (p. 17). By lynching the kitten that is disturbing his father's sleep he subverts his father's authority, and ignites a process of estrangement of which the actual writing of the autobiography is the culmination. . . .

The institution of the family, we soon discover, defines only the first environment which shapes and threatens Richard. It is merely the first universe within and against which he develops as a distinct personality. Richard must now face the racist white

South. Although no biological law binds him to it, Richard must constantly carry its culture within himself while trying to escape from it. This culture cannot be fought with knives and razors since it pervades the social world—of religion, school, and racism—in which young Richard must live and work.

External to the family and yet hardly distinguishable from it, religion comes uninvited to Richard, first in the guise of the Seventh-Day Adventist Church of his fanatical grandmother and later in the guise of the Black Methodist Church of his more moderate mother and friends. The budding strength of his personality enables Richard to resist, at first, the potent machinery of family and friends, and their attempts to save his soul:

> The hymns and sermons of God came into my heart only long after my personality had been shaped and formed by uncharted conditions of life . . . and in the end I remained basically unaffected. (p. 124)

In a later episode, however, Richard finds himself seduced by the social environment of the Methodist Church:

> I entered a new world: prim, brown, puritanical girls— black college students . . . black boys and girls. . . . I was so starved for association with people that I allowed myself to be seduced by it all. (pp. 166–67)

When a revival begins, Richard is urged to attend and join the Church: "'We don't want to push you,' they said delicately, implying that if I wanted to associate with them I would have to join" (p. 167). Much like the family, the Church embodies and sanctions a group which confronts the individual by asking him either to be a part of it or to remain alone. "It was hard to refuse," when refusal means returning to imprisonment within the family. Besieged by the preacher, the congregation, and his mother, Richard—in the company of a few other lost sheep—finds himself trapped into allegiance to the group. . . .

Walking home "limp as a rag," feeling "sullen anger and a crushing sense of shame," the newly baptized Richard has lived the nightmare which underlies the entire narrative: the domination of the group over the individual through the power of social consensus. This episode first articulates a vision which will become increasingly more pronounced throughout the autobiography. The congregation—or the tribe—merges as a powerful abstract living body which, while formed by individuals, exists in and of itself, over and against the very individuals who at some level compose it. This reified perception becomes more evident in the portrayal of two other institutions—the school and racism. It culminates with the experiences in the Communist Party—in this autobiography, the most reified of all groups.

Outside of the family, yet still in the South, while the individual's soul finds nourishment in the church, his intellect must find it in school. Central to the hero's experiences within the educational institution is the confrontation over the speech that he is to deliver as class valedictorian. In another variation of the theme "group versus individual," three groups—family, school friends, and whites—ally themselves together against the hero. Assigned to deliver the graduation speech, Richard discovers that his principal has already written one. No other student has ever refused to comply, and if he will not submit, Richard will give up the chance to teach in the school system. For Richard, however, complying with the principal means complying with the racist South: "He was tempting me, baiting me; this was the technique that snared black young minds into supporting the southern way of life" (p. 194). It means complying with his more submissive school friends—"My class mates, motivated by a desire to 'save' me, pestered me until I all but reached the breaking point,"—as well as with his family, both groups fervently opposing his determination (p. 196). Shortly before giving his own speech, the narrator remembers "I was hating my environment more each day" (p. 196).

A new and larger environment opens up for Richard the moment he steps out of school. Waiting for him is the white world with its institutions of racism, segregation, and violence. While much more powerful and threatening, this world allows Richard to distance himself from his previous environment and from its values.

> The truth was that I had—even though I had fought against it—grown to accept the value of myself that my old environment had created in me, and I had thought that no other kind of environment was possible. (p. 240)

Richard's experiences among whites illustrate various degrees of Black submission or adaptation to the "culture of terror" from which the hero will soon flee. Wright chooses two individuals in the store of his recollections to illustrate how a personality can become identical with its social environment. In Jackson, Grigg wants Richard to learn how to act "like a black" around white people; Grigg says he hates whites, yet submits completely to their authority. When he made fun of whites and began to laugh, "he covered his mouth with his hand and bent at the knees, a gesture which was unconsciously meant to conceal his excessive joy in the presence of whites" (p. 204). Similarly, in Memphis, Richard meets Shorty, "the most amazing specimen of southern Negro" (p. 248). Shorty is willing to do anything for a quarter and even lets himself be kicked by a white man after having clowned around for him in the most shameless way.

Painfully aware of the destruction of individual personality which the environment produces on both Grigg and Shorty, Wright presents Richard as the antithesis of submission and adaptation. Beaten for not saying "sir," fired for his looks, driven out of a job, forced to fight with another Black boy for the amusement of whites, Richard discovers in the "civilized" culture seeping through to him from books and magazines the sustenance which his own culture does not provide:

> From where in this southern darkness had I caught a sense of freedom? . . . The external world of whites and blacks, which was the only world that I had ever known, surely

had not evoked in me any belief in myself. The people I had met had advised and demanded submission. . . . It had been only through books. . . . Whenever my environment had failed to support or nourish me, I had clutched at books. (p. 282)

The contradictions inherent in the relationship between individual and group reach the starkest point in *American Hunger*, the second part of the autobiography. Here, the last stage of Wright's individual confrontation with the group unfolds through his relationship with the Communist Party. Unlike the family and the South, the Party represents a social organization which Richard chooses to join. However, like the family and the South, the Party provides a system of kinship and community; once again, the alternative to allegiance is isolation. . . .

The Communist Party feeds Wright's secular hunger for a sustained relationship without racism, for an intellectual light which can dissolve the epigraphic "darkness in the daytime" and the "[groping] at noonday as in the night." At the same time, the Party becomes an abstract power opposed to his personality, transcending yet subsuming all of the preceding institutions from which he fled.

The Party, much like the family, is constructed as a kinship system. Both contain a degree of "oneness" which is dearly, if fearfully, portrayed in the purge trial of Ross, another member:

Ross was one with all the members there, regardless of race or color: his heart was theirs and their hearts were his; and when a man reaches that state of *kinship* with others, that degree of *oneness*, or when a trial has made him *kin* after he has been sundered from them by wrongdoing, then he must rise and say. . . ."I'm guilty. Forgive me." (pp. 124–25, my emphasis)

Like a religion, the Party hinges around a "common vision" and notions of guilt. However, unlike religion, it relies not on "mysticism" or the "invoking of God," but rather on a "moral code that could control the conduct of men, yet it was a code that stemmed from practical living, and not from the injunctions of the supernatural" (p. 121). Control is once more in the foreground—control by the group, the environment, the society. The Party, no less than the family and the church, exacts a high toll from its members.

The similarities between the Party and the racist South are also highlighted. At Ross's trial Wright has a momentary vision of his fellow comrades as being free of racial hate and prejudice, but quickly realizes that the South has followed him yet in another guise: "I had fled men who did not like the color of my skin, and now I was among men who did not like the tone of my thoughts" (p. 119). The South has followed him in the shape of another group which isolates minority thoughts. It also has followed him as the agent of distrust and suspicion between Wright and other Blacks.

Note

12. Cited in Robert Park, "Sociological Methods of W.G. Sumner, and W.I. Thomas and F. Znaniecki," in *Methods in Social Science: A Case Book*, ed. S. Rice, (Chicago: University of Chicago Press, 1931), p. 166. Due to the time and space limits imposed upon this essay, I sacrificed in part the discussion of the Chicago School of Urban Sociology, a discussion which deserves far more attention. I often refer to the Chicago School as if it were a homogeneous entity, when, in fact, the group included as many theories and methodologies as individuals; it refers also to this intellectual school as if it were identifiable with the 1930s, when, in fact, by that time a "second generation" had already taken over. As it will soon become clear, the sociological study from which I largely draw is W.I. Thomas and F. Znaniecki, *The Polish Peasant in Europe and America*, 5 vols. (Chicago: University of Chicago Press, 1918–1920). Thomas did not belong to the second generation of sociologists, those with whom Richard Wright might have been more easily acquainted. My apology for not emphasizing more those sociologists which we know Wright had read (see note 18) is twofold: first, I was not tracing the lost map of Wright's sociological readings through the extant fragments scattered in his works; secondly, as my reading of Chicago sociologists progressed, I noticed that the focus of my concern—structure, concepts, point of view—found in *The Polish Peasant* unified within a single text many aspects of Wright's sociological constructs.

Yoshinobu Hakutani on Some Unique Elements in Richard Wright's Autobiography

But the most important distinction *Black Boy* bears as autobiography is Wright's intention to use the young self as a mask. The attitudes and sentiments expressed by the young Wright are not totally his own but represent the responses of those he called "the voiceless Negro boys" of the South.[9] Such a technique makes *Black Boy* a unique autobiography just as a similar technique makes *Native Son* a unique novel (Wright tells us that Bigger Thomas is a conscious composite portrait of numerous individual blacks he has known in his life[10]).

II

The uniqueness of Wright's autobiography can be explained in another way. Since he is a spokesman for the voiceless black youths of the South he had known in his life, he must be objective and scientific in his observations. Thus *Black Boy*, though not intended as such, is a convincing sociological study. Like sociology, it not only analyzes a social problem but offers a solution to the problem it treats. Wright's purpose is to study the way in which black life in the South was determined by its environment, and, to borrow Zola's words, his desire is to "disengage the determinism of human and social phenomena so that we may one day control and direct these phenomena."[11] Wright is constantly trying to make his investigation systematic and unbiased. He is concerned with the specific social forces in the environment of a black boy: white racism, black society, and his own family.

James Baldwin has accused Wright of his belief that "in Negro life there exists no tradition, no field of manners, no possibility of ritual or intercourse, such as may, for example, sustain the Jew even after he has left his father's house."[12] Unlike Baldwin, who grew up in a highly religious black community in Harlem, Wright in the deep South witnessed "the essential bleakness of black life in America" (p. 33). The central issue, however, is whether such human traits as, in Wright's words, "tenderness, love, honor, loyalty, and the capacity to remember" are innate in the Negro tradition, as Baldwin says, or are "fostered, won, struggled and suffered for," as Wright believed (p. 33). Elsewhere Wright tells us that he "wrote the book to tell a series of incidents strung through my childhood, but the main desire was to render a judgment on my environment. . . . That judgment was this: the environment the South creates is too small to nourish human beings, especially Negro human beings."[13] Wright, therefore, squarely places the burden of proof upon white society, contending with enough justification given in *Black Boy* that the absence of these human qualities in black people stemmed from years of white oppression.

To Wright, the effect of white oppression in the South was most visible in the black communities of the Mississippi Delta. By the time he became fourteen he was able to read and write well enough to obtain a job, in which he assisted an illiterate black insurance salesman. On his daily rounds to the shacks and plantations in the area, he was appalled by the pervasiveness of segregated life: "I saw a bare, bleak pool of black life and I hated it; the people were alike, their homes were alike, and their farms were alike" (p. 120). Such observations later infuriated not only white segregationists but many black citizens, who wrote letters to the FBI and denounced *Black Boy*. Letters called him "a black Nazi" and "one of the biggest spreaders of race hatred." Another black protester complained: "I am an American Negro and proud of it because we colored people in America have come a long way in the last seventy years. . . . We colored people don't mind the truth but we do hate lies or anything that disturb[s] our peace of mind."[14]

What had, at first, disturbed Wright was not the failure of many blacks and whites alike to see the facts of racism, but their inability to recognize malice in the minds of white racists. *Black Boy* recounts an incident in which Wright was once wrongfully accused of addressing a white employee at an optical company without using the title "Mr." Another white employee later corroborated the accusation by telling Wright: "'Didn't you call him *Pease*? If you say you didn't, I'll rip your gut string loose with this f-k-g bar, you black granny dodger! You can't call a white man a liar and get away with it!'" (p. 166). Consequently Wright was forced to leave his job. Resenting a black man's obtaining what they considered a white man's occupation, these white men deliberately created a falsehood to deny Wright a livelihood.

In retrospect, however, Wright realizes that such grudges as white men held against black men did not seem to derive from the white men themselves. He theorizes that they were not acting as individual men, but as "part of a huge, implacable, elemental design toward which hate was futile" (p. 170). Wright's autobiography does not for one moment concern itself with the theme of evil, as romantic fiction or tragic drama sometimes does.[15] *Black Boy* is intended as a sociological document rather than a novel; what such a document shows is the fact that the oppressors are as much victims of the elemental design of racism as are the oppressed. The center of Wright's interest, then, rests on deciphering this design.

In *Black Boy* Wright is continually at pains to show that white people have a preconceived notion of a Negro's place in the South: He serves them, he is likely to steal, and he cannot read or write. The tabooed subjects that Southerners refused to discuss with black men included "American white women; the Ku Klux Klan; France, and how Negro soldiers fared while there; Frenchwomen; Jack Johnson; the entire northern part of the United States; the Civil War; Abraham Lincoln; U. S. Grant; General Sherman; Catholics; the Pope; Jews; the Republican Party; slavery; social equality; Communism; Socialism; the 13th, 14th, and 15th Amendments of the Constitution" (p. 202). Sex and religion were the most accepted subjects, for they were the topics that did not require positive knowledge or self-assertion on the part of the black man. White men did not mind black men's talking about sex as long as it was not interracial. Sex was considered purely biological, and like religion it would not call for the will power of an individual. Although blacks were physically free, the South had replaced traditional slavery with a system by which their freedom of speech and movement was closely monitored and restricted. The culprit was not any individual white man; it was the complicity of white society that had allowed the design of slavery to renew itself in the twentieth-century South.

What underlies this new design of slavery? Most significantly, black men are classified as animals, a mentality inherited from the old days of slavery. Not only are black people considered to be white men's servants, but they are expected to entertain them as though blacks were animals in the zoo. Crimes perpetrated on fellow blacks are not condemned as such. Wright cites an incident in which his foreman at a company he worked for instigated antagonism between Wright and a black employee at another company so that they would try to stab each other. Wright, avoiding the trap, agreed instead to fight a boxing match to satisfy the white employees' whim. "'I suppose,'" Wright reasoned, "'it's fun for white men to see niggers fight. . . . To white men we're like dogs or cocks'" (pp. 207–208). Even killing among black men would not prick the white men's consciences. Such an attitude echoes that of the white public at the trial of Bigger Thomas for the murder of Bessie Mears, his black girlfriend, in *Native Son*.

Another degrading assumption white men hold about black men is that, since they are treated as animals, they are not supposed to possess intellectual capabilities. The reason for the young Wright's losing employment is often related to his intelligence, which poses a threat to the white man's sense of superiority. Wright points out, for instance, that some black men tried to organize themselves and petitioned their white employers for higher wages and better working conditions. But he correctly observes that such a movement was swiftly avenged by further restrictions and brutality. Throughout the book Wright continues to demonstrate the fact that Southern whites would rather have blacks who stole goods and property than blacks who were conscious, however vaguely, of the worth of their own intelligence and humanity. For Wright, racism induces black deceit and encourages black irresponsibility. Ironically, blacks are rewarded in the degree that they can make the whites feel safe and maintain their moral superiority.

Needless to say, the forces of racism have devastating effects on black life. Critics, both black and white, have complained that Wright in *Black Boy* lacks racial pride. It is true that he is critical of the black community in the South, but it is not true that he places the blame on the black community itself. His intention is to show that a racist system produced the way of life that was forced on black people. In terms of social determinism, *Black Boy* provides a literary experiment to demonstrate uniformity in Negro behavior under the influence of social forces.[16]

Most black people, he admits, do adjust to their environment for survival. But in doing so they lose individuality, self-respect, and dignity. This is perhaps the reason that Benjamin Davis, Jr., a black leftist critic, attacked Wright's portrayal of the Southern black community: "*Black Boy* says some wholly unacceptable things about the Negro's capacity for genuine emotion."[17] To Wright, however, it is the circumstances in which Negroes find themselves that cause the personalities to warp, and this in turn results in various forms of hypocritical and erratic behavior. The most striking example of this appears in an incident with an elevator boy the young Wright encountered in Memphis. The black boy, who professed that "he was proud of his race and indignant about its wrongs," never hesitated to expose his buttocks for a white man to kick so he could solicit a quarter from the white man. Wright tells us he felt "no anger or hatred, only disgust and loathing," and that he confronted this youth:

> "How in God's name can you do that?"
> "I needed a quarter and I got it," he said soberly, proudly.
> "But a quarter can't pay you for what he did to you," I said.
> "Listen, nigger," he said to me, "my ass is tough and quarters is scarce." (p. 200)

About white men's sexual exploitation of black women, Wright is as much critical of black women as of white men, because black women expect and readily condone white men's behavior.

Once a black maid who had been slapped playfully on her buttocks by a white nightwatchman told the indignant Wright who had witnessed the incident: "'They never get any further with us than that, if we don't want 'em to'" (p. 174).

Understandably such portraits of black men and women made some readers feel that Wright unduly deprived black people of their personal honor and dignity. For Ralph Ellison, Wright's autobiography lacks "high humanity," especially among its blacks. As Dan McCall correctly argues, however, "Wright is trying to show us how this gross state came about. He refuses to dress up his Negroes in an imported Sunday best because he has a far larger task before him."[18] Wright explains:

> I began to marvel at how smoothly the black boys acted out the roles that the white race had mapped out for them. Most of them were not conscious of living a special, separated, stunted way of life. Yet I knew that in some period of their growing up—a period that they had no doubt forgotten—there had been developed in them a delicate, sensitive controlling mechanism that shut off their mind and emotions from all that the white race had said was taboo. (p. 172)

One of the remarkable insights *Black Boy* offers is that social determinism takes its heaviest toll in Wright's family life. One would assume that if black boys are mistreated in society at large, they would at least be protected in their family. But in Wright's early childhood his father deserted his wife and children; not only did Wright become a casualty of the broken family, but his father himself was a victim of the racial system in the deep South. Wright observes about his father: "From the white landowners above him there had not been handed to him a chance to learn the meaning of loyalty, of sentiment, of tradition" (p. 30).

Consequently, the young Wright was subjected to the crushing blow of family antagonisms.[19] His grandmother's Seventh-Day-Adventist doctrine as practiced at home epitomizes this hostility and strife. Wright saw "more violent quarrels in our deeply religious home than in the home of a gangster, burglar, or a prostitute. . . . The naked will to power seemed always to walk in the wake of a hymn" (p. 119). While Granny held on to the helm of the family, several of Wright's uncles also attempted to administer their authority. One of them, enraged by Wright's impolite mannerisms, scolded his nephew for not acting as "the backward black boys act on the plantations"; he was ordered "to grin, hang my head, and mumble apologetically when I was spoken to" (p. 138). It seems as though black adults, subjected to racism in white society, in turn felt compelled to rule their children at home. The black adults had grown up in the world in which they were permitted no missteps in a white-dominated society. The fact that Wright's worst punishments, such as those he has given by his mother for setting fire to his grandmother's house, were inflicted by his closest relatives suggests how completely black life was dominated by white racism.

Notes

9. See "The Handiest Truth to Me to Plow Up Was in My Own Life," *P.M. Magazine*, 4 Apr. 1945, p. 3.

10. "How 'Bigger' Was Born," in *Native Son* (1940; rpt. New York: Harper & Row, 1966), p. xii.

11. "The Experimental Novel," in *Documents of Modern Literary Realism*, ed. George J. Becker (Princeton: Princeton Univ. Press, 1963), p. 181.

12. *Notes of a Native Son* (1955; rpt. New York: Bantam Books, 1968), 28.

13. "The Handiest Truth," p. 3.

14. See Addison Gayle, *Richard Wright: Ordeal of a Native Son* (Garden City, NY: Anchor Press/Doubleday, 1980), pp. 173–74. According to Gayle, Senator Bilbo of Mississippi condemned *Black Boy* on the floor of the U.S. Senate on June 7, 1945, as "the dirtiest, filthiest, lousiest, most obscene piece of writing that I have ever seen in print . . . it is so filthy and dirty . . . it comes from a Negro, and you cannot expect any better from a person of his type" (p. 173).

15. In general I agree with Dan McCall, who says: "Wright knew that all the evil could not be laid to a man. He refused to create a 'white villain.' . . . In *Black Boy* we see no villains; we do not even see a series of villains. We see men utterly helpless; varieties of foulness, stunted minds" (*The Example of Richard Wright* [New York: Harcourt, 1969], p. 128).

16. Edward Margolies observes: "Wright traps the reader in a stereotyped response—the same stereotyped response that Wright is fighting throughout the book: that is, that all Negroes are alike and react alike" (*The Art of Richard Wright* [Carbondale: Southern Illinois Univ. Press, 1969], p. 19).

17. "Some Impressions of *Black Boy*," *Daily Worker*, 1 Apr. 1945, p. 9.

18. *The Example of Richard Wright*, pp. 118–19.

19. Black Boy as autobiography can be closely compared with Angelo Herndon's *Let Me Live* (1937). Both writers depict the forces of segregation that had devastating effects on their educations and job opportunities. Both describe poverty and hunger in the plights of their families. But, while Wright grew up without his father and with his bedridden mother and hostile relatives, Herndon could rely on the traditional family loyalty—a father with trust and confidence in his son and a warmhearted, loving mother.

JENNIFER H. POULOS ON "BAD LANGUAGE" IN *BLACK BOY*

In 1945, Richard Wright published *Black Boy*,[2] an autobiographical text in which he literally curses his way through the early part of his life. A concern with the nature and use of "bad" language[3] marks *Black Boy*. Wright's deployment of bad language plays a crucial role in shaping him as an African-American artist. For *Black Boy* considers not only the development of an artist, but the conflict inherent in the very idea of becoming an African-American artist, and of gaining control over a tool—language—which traditionally barred or curtailed African-American expression.

The importance of education, and of learning to read and write in particular, is a pronounced theme in African-American literature, dating at least from the time of the slave narrative. As Frederick Douglass explained the racial politics of education through the mouth of his master: "'Learning would spoil the best nigger in the world. Now,' said he, 'if you teach that nigger ... how to read, there would be no keeping him. It would forever unfit him to be a slave.'"[4] The ability to express oneself as an educated person can alter fundamentally the identity of a slave; the struggle for self-expression is the struggle for freedom.

Thus, from slavery onward, the meaning of "bad" language doubles back on itself. "Bad" language can be good; the "obscenity" of an African-American expressing him/herself also frees African-Americans from the stereotypes imposed on them by an oppressive white culture. Such self-expression is also "bad" because it endangers the life of the African-American who disrupts the racist status quo. These contradictions underlie the slang term "bad" in African-American culture. As Tony Thorne defines the term, "bad" means "good," and originates "from the terminology of the poorest black Americans, either as simple irony or based on the assumption that what is bad in the eyes of the white establishment is good for them."[5] . . .

The African-American community understands that language is not a simple communication tool and acts with full awareness of the political uses of labeling language "good" or "bad."

To compose *Black Boy*, Richard Wright negotiated through a language fully implicated in the hierarchies of social power. As Horace Porter notes, "Wright's incredible struggle to master words is inextricably bound to his defiant quest for individual existence and expression."[7] Wright needed language to express himself but in acquiring these skills he risked becoming "bad" by definition of both African-American and white cultures. To become the artist he wanted to be, Richard Wright had to overcome the "badness" ascribed to his expression because he was African-American and avoid complicity with Western ideas of "good literature." He needed to turn "bad" and "good" into "bad" in the African-American sense. Richard Wright accomplishes this negotiation in *Black Boy* by linking literal "bad" language—dirty words, obscenities, curses—with ideas of inappropriate speech as defined by a racist society. He plays these notions off each other to redefine notions of "good" and "bad" language.

As narrator, Wright does not use direct citations of swearing frequently in the text until the younger Richard has mastered their meaning and use. When Aunt Jody catches him swearing—"'That goddam lousy bastard sonofabitching bucket!'" (*BB* 113)—Richard is in control of the terms. He may shock his family, but his use of these terms is, in a sense, appropriate and justified because the water has spilled all over him. Earlier in the text, when Richard's use of profanity is inappropriate to events, Wright represses the actual words. He does not transcribe the remarks Richard repeated in the saloon, or the text of his soap-words. When Richard tells Granny to "kiss back there," Wright suppresses profanity in euphemism. Even the foul language of the saloon patrons is absent from the text. This strategy allows Wright to claim the "badness" of the language while retaining a "good" surface, thus foiling attempts to judge his prose as inferior or obscene.

Wright places indiscriminate, inappropriate swearing in the mouths of whites. When Wright narrates his early work experiences, he reprints in detail and at length the bad language of his employers. Whites swear gratuitously and with the intention of degrading others; these people are not the laughing saloon patrons:

> "What the hell!" he snarled. "Every morning it's these damn eggs for breakfast."
> "Listen, you sonofabitch," the woman said, sitting too, "you don't have to eat 'em."
> "You might try serving some dirt," he said, and forked up the bacon.
> I felt I was dreaming. Were they like that all the time? If so, I would not stay here. A young girl came and flopped into her chair.
> "That's right, you bitch," the young man said. "Knock the food right out of my goddamn mouth."
> "You know what you can do," the girl said. (*BB* 175)

This dramatic and callous use of profanity is typical of whites and is completely inappropriate to the situation: breakfast. In a book in which a recurring theme is hunger, the young man's cavalier dismissal of a breakfast that Richard, understating the case, calls "promising" (*BB* 175) emphasizes the obscenity of the language by inflecting it through racism. Richard is chronically underfed because of poverty generated by segregation, while whites seem indifferent to the benefits they receive from the oppression of African-Americans. Wright here couples Richard's first extended experience with racism with an upsurge of bad language in the text which undercuts stereotypical definitions of the domain of "bad" language.

Wright elaborates on this concept in Richard's experiences at the optician's shop in Jackson, Mississippi. Reynolds and Pease, white lens grinders, begin to abuse Richard when he tries to learn their trade, as he had been promised when he was hired. Once Richard moves out of his place as cleaning boy and errand runner, "they changed . . . they said good morning no more. When I was just a bit slow in performing some duty, I was called a lazy black sonofabitch" (*BB* 222). Reynolds and Pease disparage black sexuality—"I heard that a nigger can stick his prick in the ground and spin around on it like a top . . . I'd give you a dime, if you did it" (*BB* 222–223)—then terrorize him into quitting. They call him a "black sonofabitch," a "granny dodger," and talk about hitting him with a "f-k-g bar" (*BB* 224–225). Racism generates profanity. Wright, using excessive amounts of bad language here, retains for himself the ability to use bad language judiciously. At the level of the text, Richard Wright is in full control of bad language.

Within the text, however, Wright links episodes of inappropriate speech to literal "bad language" to explore the badness, by definition, of all attempts of African-Americans at self-expression. The two horrific scenes which open *Black Boy*—the house fire and the hanging of the kitten—lay the groundwork for Richard Wright's determination to speak and the treachery this project involves. By their shock value, these scenes indicate that the implacable desire to speak, on the part of a black child, is dangerous and must be silenced. The opening scene of *Black Boy*, when the four-year-old Richard partially bums down the house, is rooted in the mother's warnings to Richard "to keep still," to "make no noise" (3). His childish delight in a bird "wheel[ing] past the window" yields an instinctive "glad shout" from the young boy, followed by a sharp reprimand from his mother (3). Bored and resentful of such censorship, Richard sets the curtains on fire, causing a conflagration. The results of his action silence him: "I was terrified; I wanted to scream but was afraid" (5). His revenge against his mother is effective, but he is momentarily silenced by the awareness that, without comprehending what exactly went wrong, he has committed a grievous error. Albert E. Stone reads this scene as a metaphorical first encounter with racism. Richard, who has fallen seriously ill after the fire and the beating he received for setting it, must "be kept quiet . . . [his] very life depended on it" (*BB* 7), according to the family doctor. Stone notes that "[m]edical and social prescriptions are the same: a black child in Mississippi must be taught to keep quiet, not to pry or protest."[8] Stone states that Richard's "glad shout" "is virtually the last sound of joy to issue from the boy's lips in the whole story,"[9] indicating that from this point forward Richard's speech ceases to be an unmediated expression of his relation to the world, but an interaction with a system fraught with misinterpretation, danger, and pain. Richard's desire to speak is shown to be bad, dangerous in its consequences, and ultimately life-threatening for the speaker.

Notes

2. Richard Wright, *Black Boy* (New York, 1993). Hereafter cited parenthetically in the text as *BB*. To avoid confusion, I refer to the protagonist of *Black Boy* as "Richard," and the writer as "Wright." Wright-as-narrator articulates some of Richard's experiences with greater consciousness of racial issues than Richard would have been capable of at the time.

3. In *Cursing in America* (Philadelphia, 1992), Timothy Jay divides the notion of "bad" language into 10 categories: cursing, profanity, blasphemy, taboo, obscenity, vulgarity, slang, epithets, insults and slurs, and scatology. Most of these categories make their appearance during the course of *Black Boy*. In his analysis, Jay uses the terms "cursing" and "dirty words" interchangeably to refer to inappropriate or offensive language. I follow his method, using the terms bad language, cursing and dirty words to designate inappropriate language in the text.

4. Frederick Douglass, "Narrative of the Life of Frederick Douglass, an American Slave," *The Classic Slave Narratives*, ed. Henry Louis Gates, Jr. (New York, 1987), 274.

5. Tony Thorne, "bad," in *The Dictionary of Contemporary Slang* (New York, 1990), 20.

7. Horace Porter, "The Horror and the Glory: Wright's Portrait of the Artist in *Black Boy* and *American Hunger*," in *Richard Wright: Critical Perspectives Past and Present*, eds. Henry Louis Gates, Jr. and K. A. Appiah (New York, 1993), 316.

8. Albert E. Stone, "The Childhood of the Artist—Louis Sullivan and Richard Wright," *Autobiographical Occasions and Original Acts* (Philadelphia, 1982), 128.

9. Ibid, 125.

ROBERT FELGAR ON A CULTURAL READING OF *BLACK BOY*

A particularly effective way of unlocking the assumptions implicit in *Black Boy* is through the lens of cultural critique, a way of reading a text that challenges what writers and their audiences often take for granted as natural rather than human constructions. For instance, in *Beloved*, Toni Morrison assumes that it goes without saying that a black man cannot be heroic and gay, which suggests her uncritical acceptance of a cultural norm over something that is actually the case. Or, to take another example, the nineteenth-century British novelist Thomas Hardy, in *Tess of the D'Urbervilles*, never questions the assumption that happiness for his heroine lies in a heterosexual relationship within the institution of marriage. Similarly, Wright accepts in his autobiography a set of axioms about social class, race, and gender that can be profitably examined, as opposed to merely accepted or ignored altogether. In making assumptions, or in being the product of them, Wright is doing what we all inevitably do when trying to make sense of the world. But cultural critique can make us aware of our assumptions, which in turn can then be subjected to analytical scrutiny.

Unrecognized assumptions about social class are everywhere in *Black Boy*. For example, although Wright despised the black middle class, he was evidently no fan of the black lower class either, for he was deeply concerned that his readers not think he could end up like his father, a "black peasant." He seems to believe that this would be a horrific fate, one to be avoided at any cost, a kind of social hell. A dubious social perspective also informs Wright's reactions to the black families he sees when he works as an assistant to an insurance agent named Brother Nance: "Many of the naive black families bought their insurance from us because they felt that they were connecting themselves with something that would make their children 'write'n speak lak dat pretty boy from Jackson'" (160). He later refers to such people as "walleyed yokels" (161), an unfortunate phrase that suggests Wright's social prejudices. He is intellectually aware that social classes are not natural entities because at one point in *Black Boy* he uses the phrase "the artificial status of race and class" (218), but this intellectual awareness about artificial social distinctions does not regulate his feelings about social class.

Race- and gender-based assumptions can also be discovered throughout *Black Boy*. At the end of Chapter 1, for instance, the narrator observes that his father had not been handed a chance to learn about loyalty, sentiment, and tradition by the white landowners. The reader might well ask why Wright's father could not have learned about these values from the black community, which was just as knowledgeable about them as the white community; however, Wright may sometimes see his own community through white eyes. The most notorious example of Wright's uncritical deployment of race-based assumptions is the passage early in Chapter II, where the narrator mulls "over the strange absence of real kindness in Negroes" and contends that black people "had never been allowed to catch the full spirit of Western civilization" (43). African Americans are as kind as anybody else, and they have developed their own cultural traditions out of the intersection of African and European cultures, but Wright may have so internalized the perspective of the majority culture that he cannot see its own limitations, anymore than people now can see without blind spots. The same Richard Wright who can acknowledge the "artificial status of race and class" (218) in the middle of *Black Boy*, and so is not completely in the grip of the notion of white as the norm, only a little later refers to "a pale yellow" African American who has gonorrhea and was proud of that fact, a reference that may betray intraracial racism in the narrator. In a society as race-bound as the United States, though, it may be asking too much of anyone to see through all its racial deceptions. Also, one should give Wright some credit for his honesty about the issue of race: not everyone, for example, would write, "I felt—but only temporarily—that perhaps the whites were right, that Negroes were children and would never grow up" (431). This remark comes out of his temporary frustration with black actors who appear in a play the public might not like. The reader should also consider that everyone, including him or herself is inevitably a product of a particular time and place. This fact does not justify Wright's attitude toward the actors but may help to explain it.

In addition to assumptions governing Wright's attitudes toward race and social class, there are gender-based suppositions that can be detected throughout *Black Boy*. It seems odd, for instance, for Wright to refer to his adult Aunt Jody as a "girl" (104), and it is embarrassing to read that Granny and Aunt Addie became so hostile toward him that they ordered him to wash and iron his own clothes, as if such work were the ultimate debasement. In one church he attended, he notes the presence of "wobbly-bosomed black and yellow church matrons" and "skinny old maids" (178), women he looks at but not with. More troubling, perhaps, is an incident involving a young black woman Wright observes as a white policeman slaps her on the buttocks; when Wright asks her how she can stand that kind of treatment, she replies that it does not matter. In response to her comment that he would have been a fool if he had done something about it, he tells her he would have been, meaning he would have been a fool to try to do something for her. She misses the point, according to the narrator, but we may wonder if Wright does not miss the point when he gives no consideration to why she might tolerate disrespectful treatment from a white man: doing anything else could have resulted in horrible consequences to her and to Wright. His attitude toward the white waitresses he works with in Chicago may also reveal a failure of empathy and imagination on his part: the reader should question why it is necessarily so bad that the "words of their souls were the syllables of popular songs" (321). Equally disturbing is his reference to a woman he dislikes for regarding him as an Uncle Tom: "a huge, fat, black woman" (432).

The worst combination for Wright is a poor, black woman because that combination embodies his deepest anxieties about social class, race, and gender (but we should keep in mind that Bessie Mears, in *Native Son*, while an example of this category, nevertheless points out to Bigger Thomas that the fact that whites have killed many blacks, does not justify his killing Mary Dalton). In *Black Boy*, the young black woman with whom Wright has sex in exchange for his paying her insurance premiums (340–43) is probably the best example of this phenomenon: not only is she poor, black, and a woman, but she is also an illiterate obsessed with the notion of seeing a circus. Wright finds her beyond his understanding because she differs so much from him that he cannot identify with her. But then, why sleep with what is perplexing and without value? And what does such a relationship suggest about Wright?

Like anybody else, Wright reflects many of the unexamined assumptions of a particular time and place: his attitudes toward black women in his autobiography are far from unique; this is not to justify but to explain them. And it is also pertinent to consider that because one is oneself a victim of prejudice, it hardly follows that one will be any less a victimizer than anyone else. Nor does a cultural reading of *Black Boy* support a sense of moral and/or intellectual superiority on the part of the reader, but it does open up the book in revealing ways that can deepen our understanding of it, and of the author and times that produced it.

Wright represents and examines the most concrete and pivotal aspects of the culture of social-death and the subjugating mechanisms of Jim Crow society in those portions of *Black Boy* that depict his life from the end of his formal education, May 1925, to his departure from the South, November 1927. As he enters the labor market, working at various odd jobs, he finds himself subject to various forms of violence, all of which hint at more decisive forms if they should become necessary. When he is bitten by the guard dog at his workplace, his complaints succeed only in provoking the response that blacks are incapable of really being hurt by a dog. When he forgets to address white boys as sir, he is hit on the head with a bottle and thrown off a moving car. His assailants consider themselves benign teachers: had he made that mistake with other white men, they insist, he might have quickly become "a dead nigger" (174). Such routine brutality seems to disturb Wright less than the threat of more serious violence, which forces him to curb his professional ambition, or the responses from whites that demand a submission so complete that it implicitly calls for the effective erasure of his consciousness of racism and its political valences. Two episodes in particular reveal these conditions, demands, and restrictions: the unsuccessful attempt by the "Yankee" owner of an optical factory to allow Richard to acquire skills in the optical business and the implicit demands by a grocery store owner that Richard erase all elements of dignity from his tone of voice in order to retain his menial job.

The Southern white employees in the optical factory who are supposed to teach him the requisite skills apparently resent the owner's attempts at racial desegregation of the profession and, fabricating a charge for which they can beat or even kill Richard, force him to resign. The fabricated charge reveals that, in addition to professional segregation and economic advantage, the entire timocratic nature of Southern racist society is at stake. The charge puts Richard in a double bind: one of the workers, Reynolds, accuses Wright of not using the appellation *Mr.* when referring to the other white man, Pease. Before Wright can even respond to this charge, Reynolds warns him that, if he denies the allegation, he will be calling Reynolds a liar. Thus, by either accepting or refuting the charge, Wright violates a cardinal rule of the Southern timocracy: a black man can never challenge the honor of a white. This ritual, accompanied by a beating and the threat of death, succeeds in enforcing all aspects of the syndrome of social-death. First, Richard is forced to acknowledge the white man as a "master" ("Mister") and, by implication, himself as a slave. Second, he has to relinquish all personal dignity, all sense of honor, to his white assailants. And, finally, in agreeing to resign, he has to accept both the death of his professional ambition and, by implication, his own social-death; he must, in a sense, commit suicide: as one of the white workers tells Richard, "If I was a nigger, I'd kill myself" (*Black Boy*, 877).[9] The suggestion of suicide accompanied by the threat of lynching is, thus, designed to teach Richard that his embrace of his social-death must be a "voluntary" act, the equivalent of suicide, in which the subject becomes the agent of his own demise.

In agreeing to resign, Richard allows the prospect of actual-death to control, at least temporarily, his conduct, if not his ultimate goals. While he is temporarily defeated, his meditation on and analysis of the final episode in this defeat brilliantly illuminates some of the underlying psychopolitical dynamics of this process of subjection. In his attempt to investigate the causes of Richard's resignation, the "Yankee" owner exhorts him, in front of Pease and Reynolds, to identify his assailant, but Richard is unable to speak: "An impulse to speak rose in me and died with the realization that I was facing a wall that I would never breech. I tried to speak several times and could make no sounds. I grew tense and tears burnt my cheeks" (*Black Boy*, 183). As Wright's subsequent remarks make clear, he weeps, not simply for the end of this particular professional ambition or because his dignity has been wounded, but, more important, because of his "complicity" in his defeat: this encounter, he says, left "[me] drenched in shame, naked to my soul. The whole of my being felt violated, *and I knew that my own fear had helped to violate it*" (184; emphasis added). Wright's remarks about the role of fear in his "self-violation" begin to reveal the interlocking psychopolitical mechanisms that constitute the process of subjection in a racialized Jim Crow society that relies on the threat of death as its primary coercive tool.

Clearly, at the sociopolitical level, the mechanism requires, as the hint of suicide implies, that the individual must so effectively "internalize" the external, social boundaries that he comes to restrict himself "voluntarily." Racist hegemony seeks to inform the very "self-conception" of the prospective "black boy" in such a way that the subject will become identical to the limited view of him that the ideological apparatus itself has constructed; indeed, the external construction of the subject should, ideally, coincide with his "self-construction." No luxury of choice is available in this process of self-construction; rather, hegemony forces the developing black individual to accommodate himself to the very absence of choice, enforced by the threat of death, and to perceive this absence not as the historical product of social relations but as a natural and even metaphysical fact of "life."

However, on the *psycho*political register, Wright's remarks about the self-violation produced by the fear of death demonstrate that the shadow of death frills not just between the world and the self but between the different psychic agencies that collectively constitute the subject: it falls between will and desire, on the one hand, and ambition, on the other; it falls between self-regard and a sense of dignity or honor, on the one hand, and fear, on the other. What Wright's remarks imply in this regard needs to be clarified: effective agency of the subject evidently shifts from the side of will and desire to the side of fear so that the latter is able to overcome and negate the combined forces of the former. This process of subjectification thus produces a subject deeply divided against himself, alienated from his telos, and, paradoxically, "empowered" as an agent in his own "e(masculine)ation."

Note

9. In fact, this remark is part of a passage that Wright substituted for one that the Book of the Month Club found objectionable. The original passage, restored in the Library of America edition (see *Later Works*, 180), focuses on disparaging remarks made by Reynolds about the mythical size of black penises, remarks that castrate the black male subject at the same time that they endow him with superhuman sexual potency. Wright's substitution of the dialectic of death for the political economy of racialized virility/castration raises some very interesting issues, which must be taken up elsewhere, but which are also partly examined in my analysis of *The Long Dream*.

Works by Richard Wright

"The Voodoo of Hell's Half-Acre," in the *Southern Register*, 1924.

Uncle Tom's Children, 1938.

Native Son, 1940.

Twelve Million Black Voices, 1941.

Black Boy, 1945.

The Outsider, 1953.

Savage Holiday, 1954.

Black Power, 1954.

The Color Curtain: A Report on the Bandung Conference, 1956.

Pagan Spain, 1957.

White Man, Listen!, 1957.

The Long Dream, 1958.

Eight Men, posthumously published, 1961.

Lawd Today, posthumously published, 1963.

Annotated Bibliography

Andrews, William L., and Douglas Taylor, eds. *Richard Wright's "Black Boy (American Hunger)": A Casebook*. Oxford and New York: Oxford University Press, 2003.

This relatively recent volume begins with an introduction to the historical background to the still-disputed issues *Black Boy* has raised over the years. The question of how authentically representational the work is begins with Wright's own stated purpose of speaking for the voiceless and continues with substantial challenges to that view. Another critical question concerns the veracity of the autobiography—whether Wright's addition of fictional elements undermines its value as a document of growing up black in the South. The selected essays include four from the time of *Black Boy*'s publication, but most are sufficiently recent to benefit from changes and developments in the way literature is read and analyzed.

Bakish, David. *Richard Wright*. New York: Frederick Ungar Publishing Company, 1973.

David Bakish's study of Richard Wright is a straightforward introduction to the author's life. The writing is accessible, a chronology is provided, and the events in Wright's life with biographical significance are grouped by years and locations.

Butler, Robert J., ed. *The Critical Response to Richard Wright*. Westport, Conn., and London: Greenwood Press, 1995.

This study of Wright's major novels traces and examines the criticism each work received both when it first appeared and later after different perspectives had emerged. Especially valuable are the reviews black writers offer of other significant black writers. A substantial chronology is also included.

Fabre, Michel. *The Unfinished Quest of Richard Wright*. New York: William Morrow & Company, Inc., 1973.

Although comprehensive studies of Wright, his work, and historical period have been more recently published, Fabre's biography continues to be regarded as a substantial contribution to understanding Wright's life. Fabre was among the first Wright scholars to document the discrepancies between Wright's account of certain events in his life and objective records and reports. Most of this study focuses on the second half of Wright's life. It is clearly written and includes almost 50 illustrations.

Felgar, Robert. *Student Companion to Richard Wright.* Westport, Conn., and London: Greenwood Press, 2000.

This volume is intended for students new to Wright's work and life. It includes a brief biography and chapters devoted to each of Wright's major works.

Gates, Henry Louis, Jr. *The Signifying Monkey: A Theory of African-American Literary Criticism.* New York and Oxford: Oxford University Press, 1988.

This study of African and African-American vernacular traditions and their influence on the potential for authentic black literature and culture received high praise when it first appeared and continues to be regarded as a seminal book. Its significance lies in the legitimacy it gives to black writers to draw on their own traditions of speech and language and to create a newly relevant and distinctive black voice that speaks for itself.

Gayle, Addison. *Richard Wright: Ordeal of a Native Son.* Garden City, N.Y.: Anchor Press/Doubleday, 1980.

Richard Wright thought of himself as a political activist as well as a novelist, and this biography of his life emphasizes his political activities in the United States and in Europe. Gayle's discussion of Wright's work focuses largely on the political writings—*Black Power, The Color Curtain, Pagan Spain,* and *White Man, Listen!*

Hakutani, Yoshinobu. *Richard Wright and Racial Discourse.* Columbia, Mo., and London: University of Missouri Press, 1996.

This study of Richard Wright looks at his work as a seminal contribution to the racial discourse in America. The early novels concentrated on life in the United States, but after his self-imposed exile to Europe, Wright enlarged his vision to include analysis of third world countries. In his preface, the author explains his intention to look at Wright's work in the context of writers from other cultures. Hakutani also devotes a chapter to Wright's poetic achievement, looking particularly at many of the 4,000 haiku the author composed at the end of his life.

————, ed. *Critical Essays on Richard Wright*. Boston: G.K. Hall & Co., 1982.

The essays collected in this volume are organized according to the genre they discuss; there is commentary on Wright's fiction, nonfiction, poetry, and general issues such as racism, the Communist Party, French existentialism, and his personal relationships with other black writers. Essays on Wright by James Baldwin and Ralph Ellison are two of the hallmarks of this volume.

JanMohamed, Abdul R. *The Death-Bound-Subject: Richard Wright's Archaeology of Death*. Durham, N.C., and London: Duke University Press, 2005.

JanMohamed's study of Wright begins with the observation that in his first three fictional works—two novels and a collection of five short stories—no fewer than 20 violent deaths are recorded, some of them especially gruesome. The author recognizes the inhibitions surrounding discussions of death but asserts that a study of Wright's particular preoccupation yields new insights into his life and work. JanMohamed uses the term *death-bound-subject* to identify those people whose lives are formed from infancy by a persistent and overarching sense of imminent death. After an introduction discussing in general terms the concepts informing his study, the author devotes a chapter to each of the novels. A productive reading of this work requires familiarity with advanced psychoanalytic theories.

Joyce, Ann Joyce. *Richard Wright's Art of Tragedy*. Iowa City: University of Iowa Press, 1986.

Although the author's emphasis in this study of Richard Wright is on *Native Son* and the character of Bigger Thomas, her perspective on Wright's work helps in understanding *Black Boy* as well. Joyce's reading of Wright focuses more on the elements of tragedy than other critics have, and although her insights do not negate the political and cultural importance in the writings, they add to a more complex understanding of the dimensions present in Wright's work.

Kinnamon, Kenneth. *Richard Wright: An Annotated Bibliography of Criticism and Commentary, 1983–2003*. Jefferson, N.C., and London: McFarland & Company, Inc., 2006.

In 1972, Kinnamon published *The Emergence of Richard Wright*, a study that focused on *Native Son* and Wright's proletarian writings. In 1988, he published *A Richard Wright Bibliography*, which covered the years 1933 through 1982. This new volume reflects the expanded interest in Wright's life but, more importantly, in the relatively recent commentary directed at the artistic qualities of his writing. Arranged by years, the volume includes 8,660 entries of substantial as well as brief references to the writer's life and work. The book is an indispensable resource for serious students of Richard Wright.

Macksey, Richard, and Frank E. Moorer, eds. *Richard Wright: A Collection of Critical Essays*. Englewood Cliffs, N.J.: Prentice-Hall, Inc., 1984.

The editors of this volume acknowledge the huge number of essays on Wright that began appearing in the decade preceding its publication; they have, as a result, been forced to choose representatives of three categories of criticism: discussions of Wright's background, especially his moves to Chicago and New York; analysis of Wright's best-known novel, *Native Son*; and exploration of the different ways the tenets of existentialism were manifested in his writings.

Reilly, John M. *Richard Wright: The Critical Reception*. New York: Burt Franklin & Co., Inc., 1978.

This collection of reviews of Wright's work emphasizes the immediate response to each publication rather than assessments that have emerged through the years. Some of the reviewers are well-established writers such as James Baldwin and literary critics such as Lionel Trilling, but most were lesser-known writers for the major daily newspapers and small journals. The reviews are arranged chronologically and grouped by the work being reviewed. This volume is a useful guide for new and advanced students interested in the history of Wright's critical reception.

Relyea, Sarah. *Outsider Citizens: The Remaking of Postwar Identity in Wright, Beauvoir, and Baldwin*. New York and London: Routledge, 2006.

This study draws on the insights of psychoanalysis, feminism, existentialism, and racial and cultural issues; as such, it is best read after acquiring familiarity with the complex issues raised by these writers. The notion of *double consciousness*, a term from the writings of W.E.B. Du Bois, is the foundation for what is called the "alienated consciousness" or the "outsider identity." As writers conscious of being "outsiders," Richard Wright, Simone de Beauvoir, and James Baldwin focused on the process and structure of identity formation within that context.

Rowley, Hazel. *Richard Wright: The Life and Times*. New York: Henry Holt and Company, 2001.

This lengthy and substantial biography draws on and extends the work already done by Michel Fabre (previously cited in this section). The writing is accessible and sometimes resembles a narrative, as Rowley follows Wright from his Mississippi cotton-field origins to his place of burial in France.

Ward, Jerry W., Jr., and Robert J. Butler, eds. *The Richard Wright Encyclopedia*. Westport, Conn. and London: Greenwood Press, 2008.

This 447-page volume covers a wealth of topics related to Richard Wright. The categorized subjects include: publishing names and information; awards, conferences and historical/ political events; African-American culture; nonpolitical events; film and photography; genres of literature; magazines and newspapers; people; places; works by Wright; drama and film;

essays and manuscripts; collections; poems; short fiction; introductions and forewords; and other writers and their works. An introduction deals mainly with biographical information. This is an excellent resource for students interested in the life, work, and times of Richard Wright.

Williams, John A. *The Most Native of Sons: A Biography of Richard Wright*. Garden City, New York: Doubleday & Company, Inc., 1970.

Williams divides his biography of Wright into three sections: his early years in Mississippi; his flight to the North, especially Chicago and New York City; and his period of exile in Europe. The book adopts a narrative style and is accessible for the beginning student. The primary source of information about Wright's life remains *Black Boy*; there are no additional sources of information cited and no footnotes.

Contributors

Harold Bloom is Sterling Professor of the Humanities at Yale University. He is the author of 30 books, including *Shelley's Mythmaking, The Visionary Company, Blake's Apocalypse, Yeats, A Map of Misreading, Kabbalah and Criticism, Agon: Toward a Theory of Revisionism, The American Religion, The Western Canon*, and *Omens of Millennium: The Gnosis of Angels, Dreams, and Resurrection. The Anxiety of Influence* sets forth Professor Bloom's provocative theory of the literary relationships between the great writers and their predecessors. His most recent books include *Shakespeare: The Invention of the Human*, a 1998 National Book Award finalist, *How to Read and Why, Genius: A Mosaic of One Hundred Exemplary Creative Minds, Hamlet: Poem Unlimited, Where Shall Wisdom Be Found?*, and *Jesus and Yahweh: The Names Divine.* In 1999, Professor Bloom received the prestigious American Academy of Arts and Letters Gold Medal for Criticism. He has also received the International Prize of Catalonia, the Alfonso Reyes Prize of Mexico, and the Hans Christian Andersen Bicentennial Prize of Denmark.

W.E.B. Du Bois (1868–1963) was a teacher, writer, historian, sociologist, and a devoted civil rights activist. His best-known work is *The Souls of Black Folk.* One of Du Bois's most seminal ideas was the notion of "double consciousness," by which he meant the experience of distorted identity suffered by black Americans as they "see" themselves simultaneously as agents of their own lives and as caught in the stereotyping and demeaning "white gaze."

Isidor Schneider was a Ukrainian immigrant to the United States who became involved in newspaper publishing and writing. He was an editor of *New Masses* and was associated with the startup of small magazines such as *The Dial* and *The Transition*. He also published *The American Caravan*.

120

Lionel Trilling was a distinguished American cultural critic who wrote for many publications including the *Partisan Review*. Because he insisted on the analytical importance of cultural and political issues in literature, he made a famous break with the New Critics school of criticism. Trilling taught at Harvard and Columbia universities. Among his best-known works are *The Liberal Imagination* (1950) and *The Opposing Self* (1955).

Ralph Ellison (1914–1994) was a novelist and activist. His best-known work is *Invisible Man* (1952). He was encouraged by Richard Wright and, like Wright, wrote for *New Masses*. Ellison made the memorable remark: "Literature is colorblind."

George E. Kent has been a professor of English at the University of Chicago. His published work includes studies of Ralph Ellison, William Faulkner, Gwendolyn Brooks, and James Baldwin. He is the author of *Blackness and the Adventure of Western Culture*.

Horace A. Porter has been a professor in the English department at Dartmouth College. He has contributed articles to *American Scholar* and the *Journal of Negro History*.

Carla Cappetti is on the faculty of the women's studies program at City College of New York.

Yoshinobu Hakutani teaches in the English department at Kent State University where he is also a University Distinguished Scholar. He has written and edited many books including *Richard Wright and Racial Discourse* and *The City in African American Literature*.

Jennifer H. Poulos teaches in the English department at Emory University in Atlanta.

Robert Felgar has written extensively on *Native Son* and *Black Boy*. He is professor of English at Jacksonville State

University in Florida. In 1998, he published *Understanding Richard Wright's "Black Boy."*

Abdul R. JanMohamed teaches in the English department at the University of California at Berkeley. He has contributed articles to the journals *Critical Inquiry* and *Whither Marxism* (1994). He is the author of *Manichean Aesthetics: The Politics of Literature in Colonial Africa* and co-editor of *The Nature and Context of Minority Literature.*

Acknowledgments

W.E.B. Du Bois, "Richard Wright Looks Back." From *The Critical Response to Richard Wright*, edited by Robert J. Butler, pp. 65–68. Published by Greenwood Press. Copyright © 1995 by Robert J. Butler. Used with permission of the David Graham Du Bois Trust.

Isidor Schneider, "One Apart," originally published in *New Masses* 54, April 3, 1945: 23–24. From *Richard Wright: The Critical Reception*, edited by John M. Reilly, pp. 149–51. Copyright © 1978 Burt Franklin & Co., Inc.

Lionel Trilling, "A Tragic Situation." From *Richard Wright: The Critical Reception*, edited by John M. Reilly, pp. 151–53. Copyright © 1978 Burt Franklin & Co., Inc. Reprinted with permission from the April 17, 1945, issue of *The Nation*. For subscription information, call 1-800-333-8536. Portions of each week's *Nation* magazine can be accessed at http://www.thenation.com

Ralph Ellison, "Richard Wright's Blues." Originally appeared in *Antioch Review* 5, no. 2 (Summer 1945): 198–211, copyright 1945 by Antioch Review, Inc. Reprinted in *Critical Essays on Richard Wright*, pp. 201–04. Published by G. K. Hall & Co. Copyright © 1982 by Yoshinobu Hakutani.

George E. Kent, "Richard Wright: Blackness and the Adventure of Western Culture." From *Richard Wright: A Collection of Critical Essays*, edited by Richard Macksey and Frank E. Moorer, pp. 38–41. Copyright © 1984 by Prentice-Hall, Inc. Originally published in the *CLA Journal* and used by permission of the College Language Association.

Horace A. Porter, "The Horror and the Glory: Richard Wright's Portrait of the Artist." From *Richard Wright: A Collection of Critical Essays*, edited by Richard Macksey and Frank E. Moorer, pp. 56–65. Copyright © 1984 by Prentice-Hall, Inc.

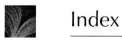

Index